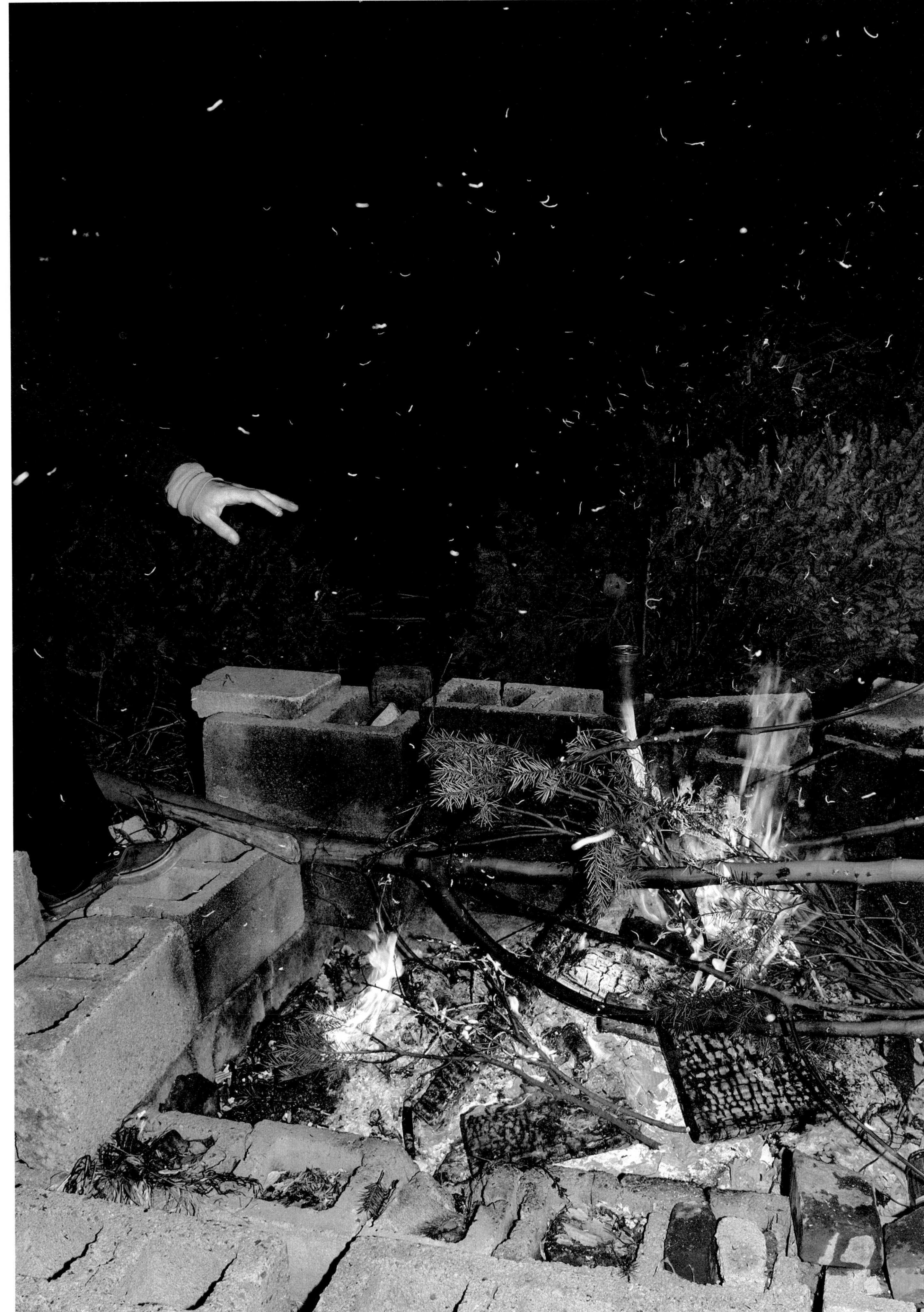

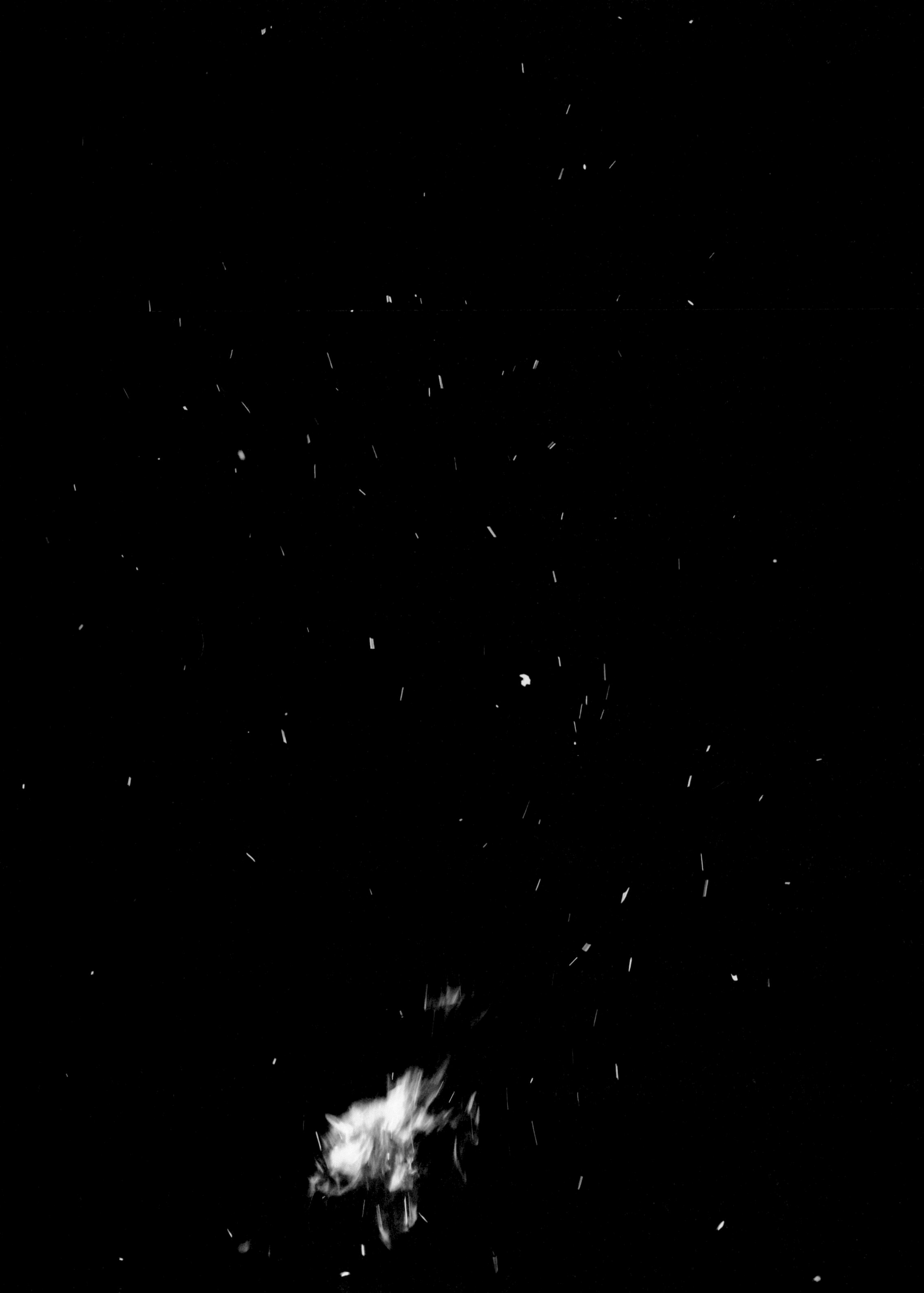

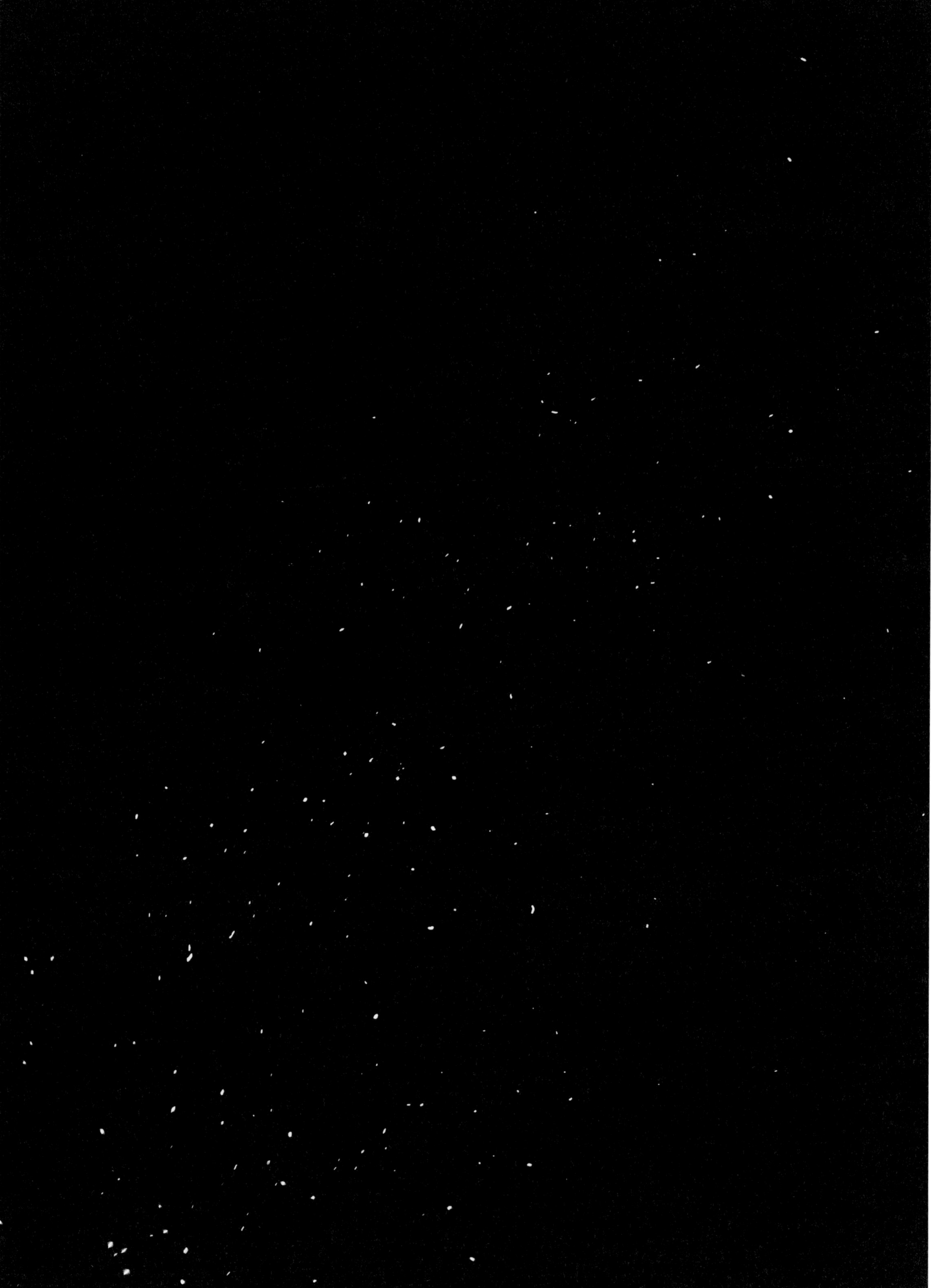

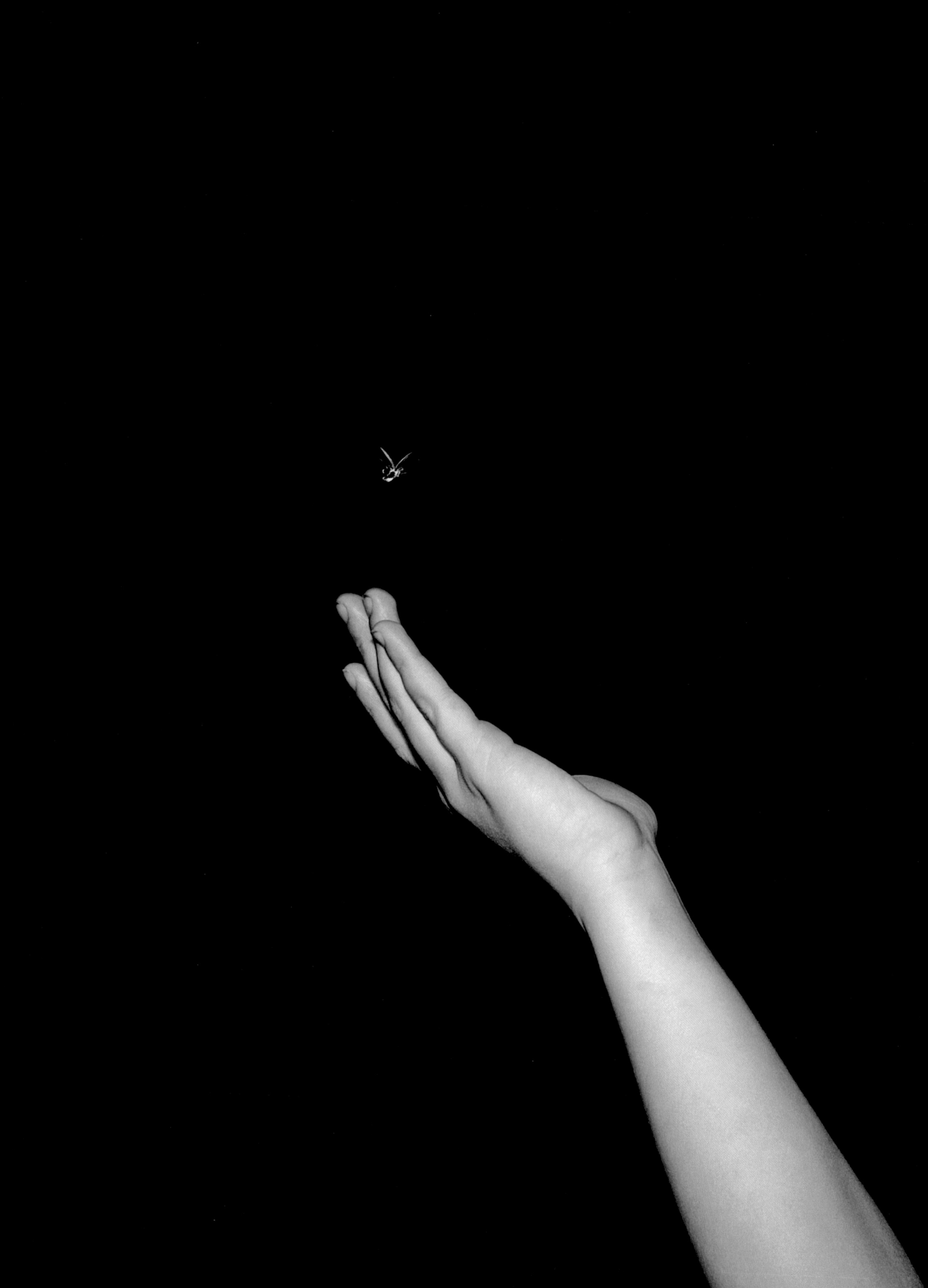

THE GROUP FOR MUTUAL IMPROVEMENT

JORDAN BAUMGARTEN

GOST

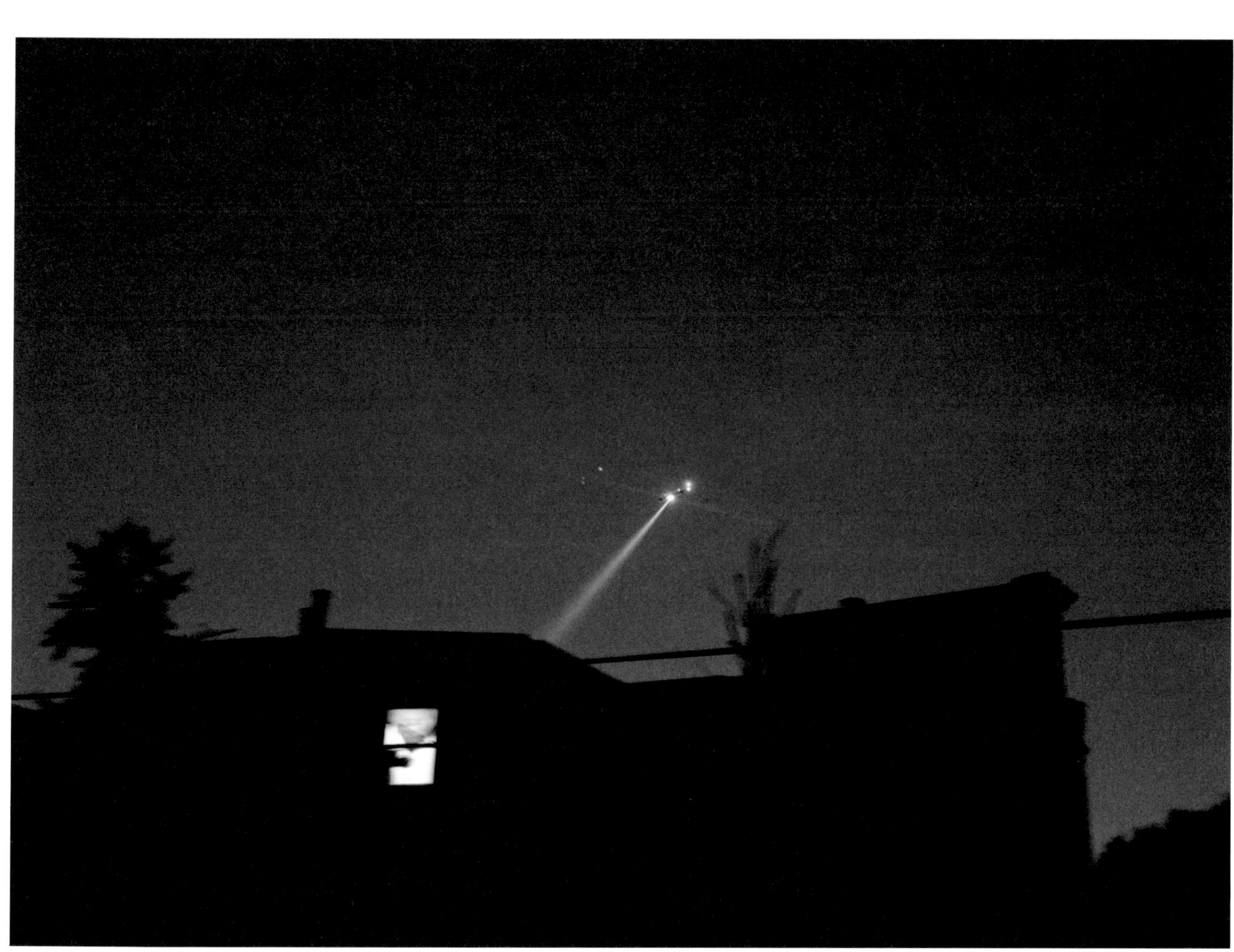

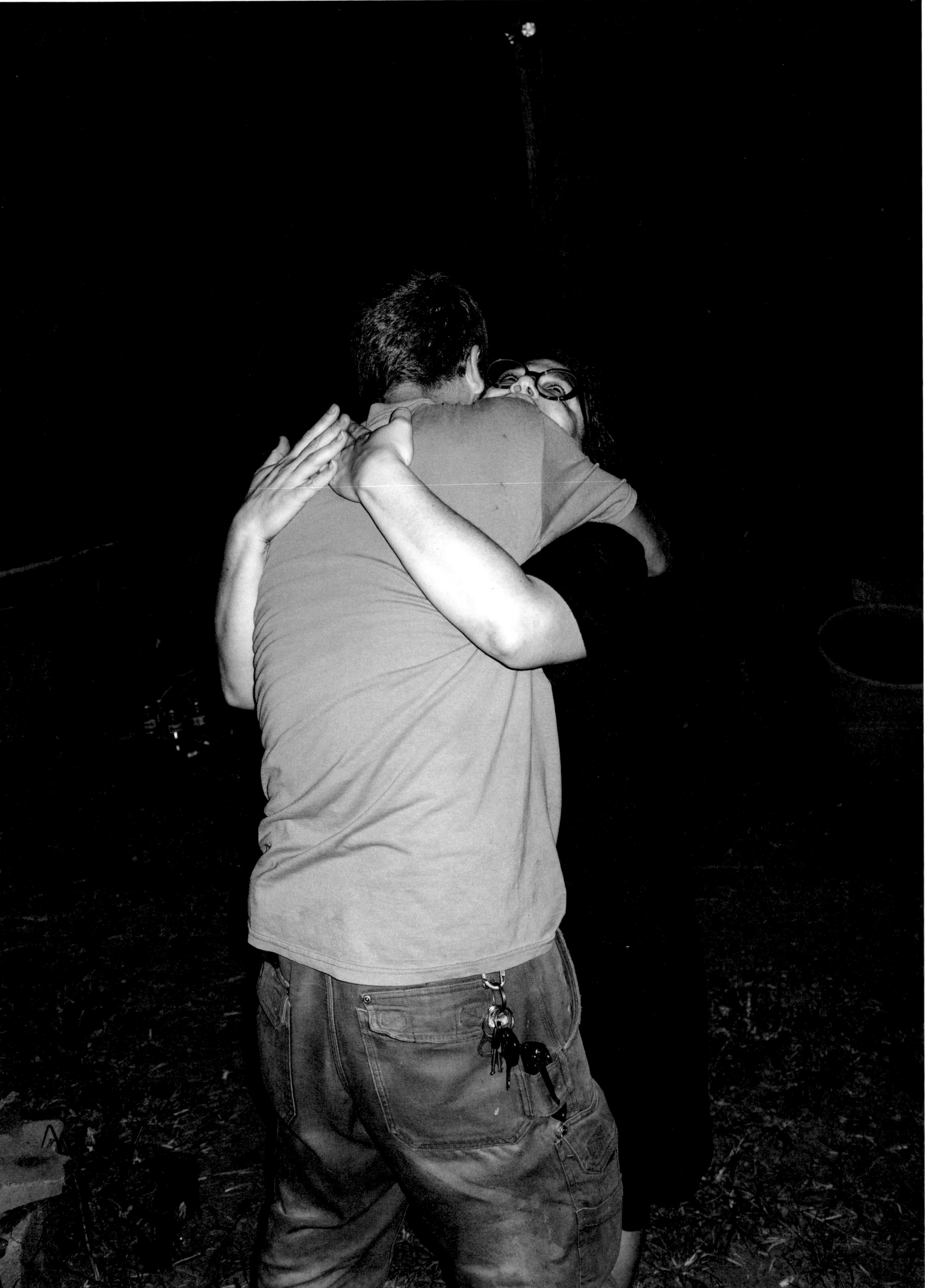

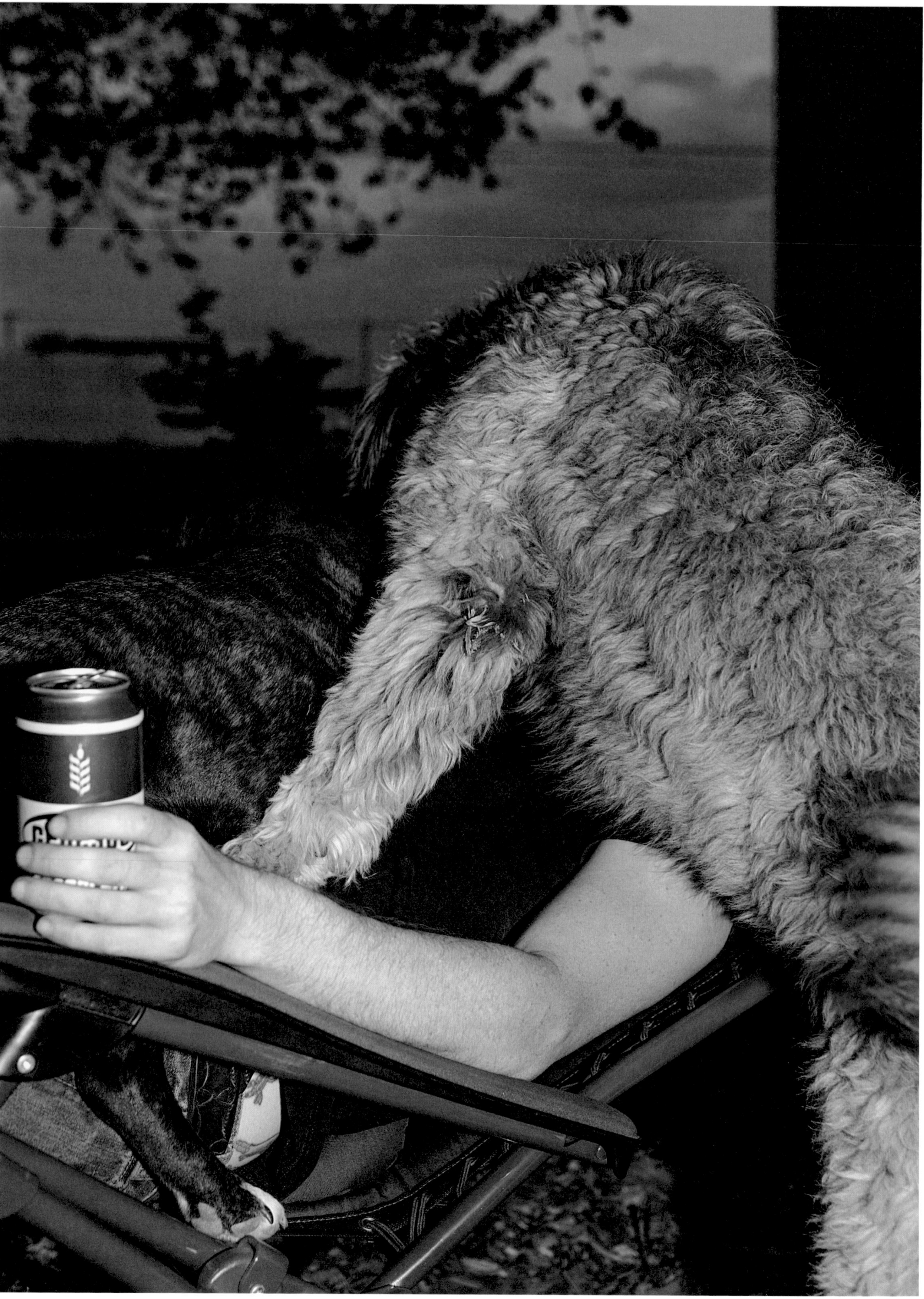

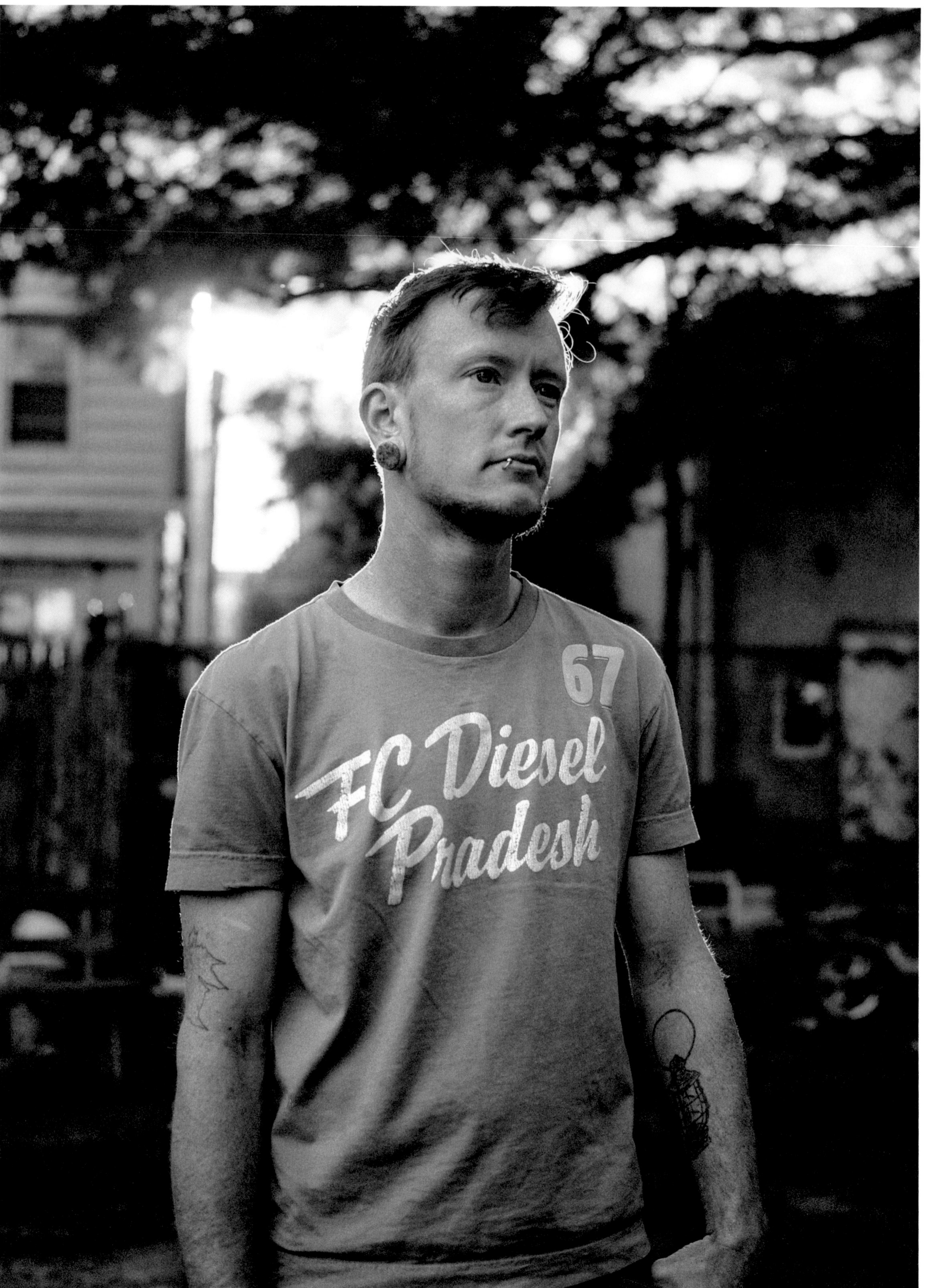
67
FC Diesel
Pradesh

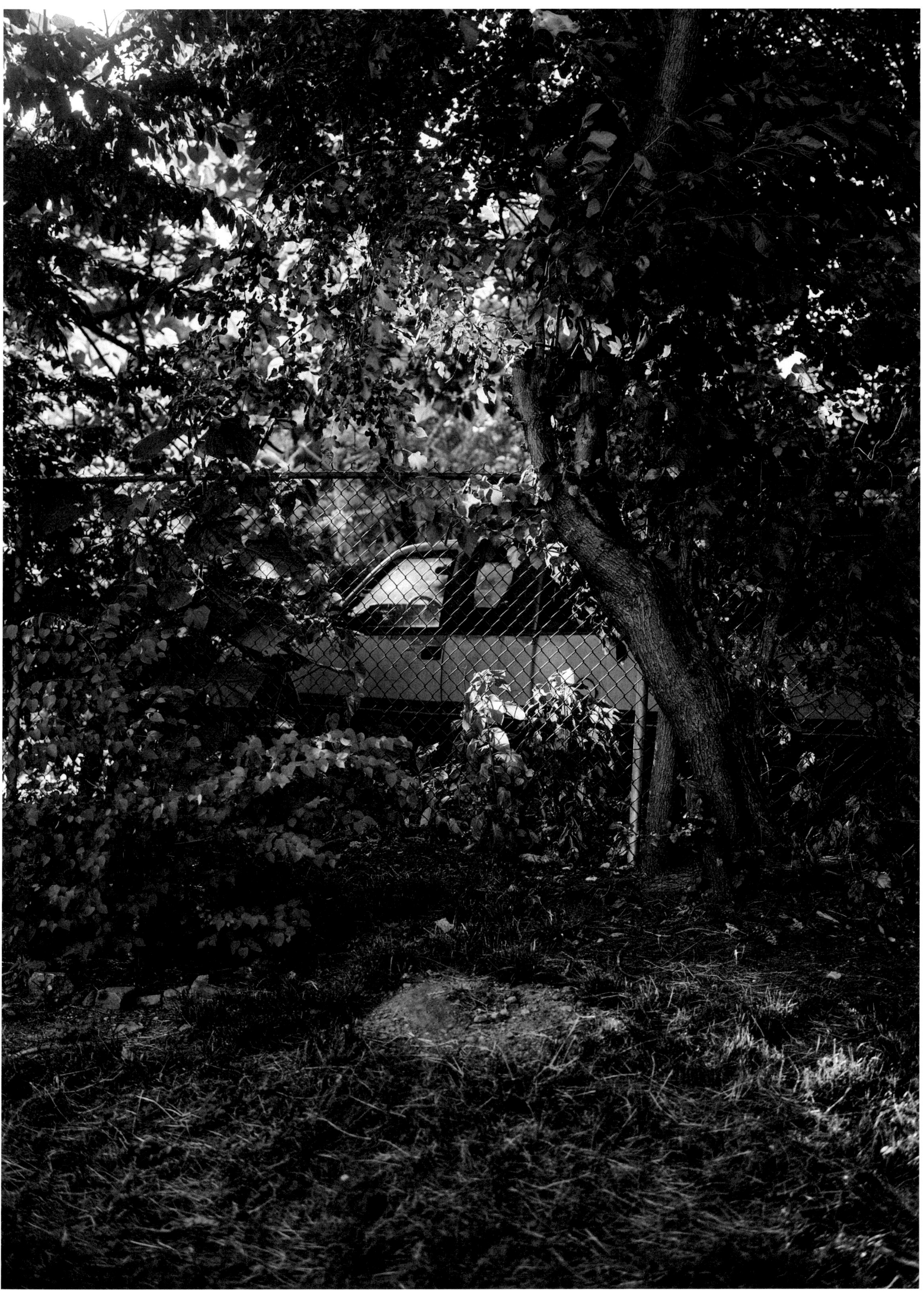

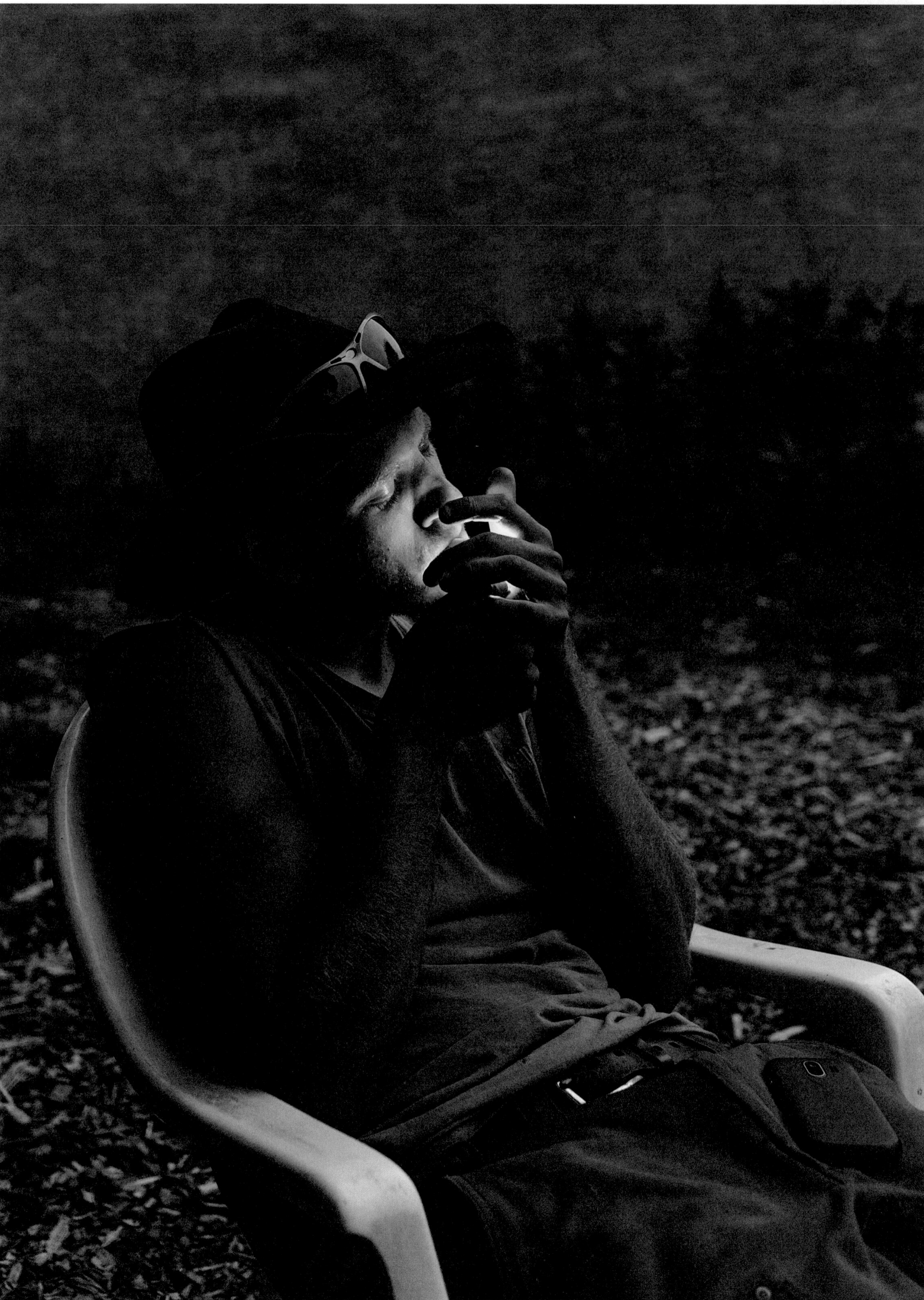

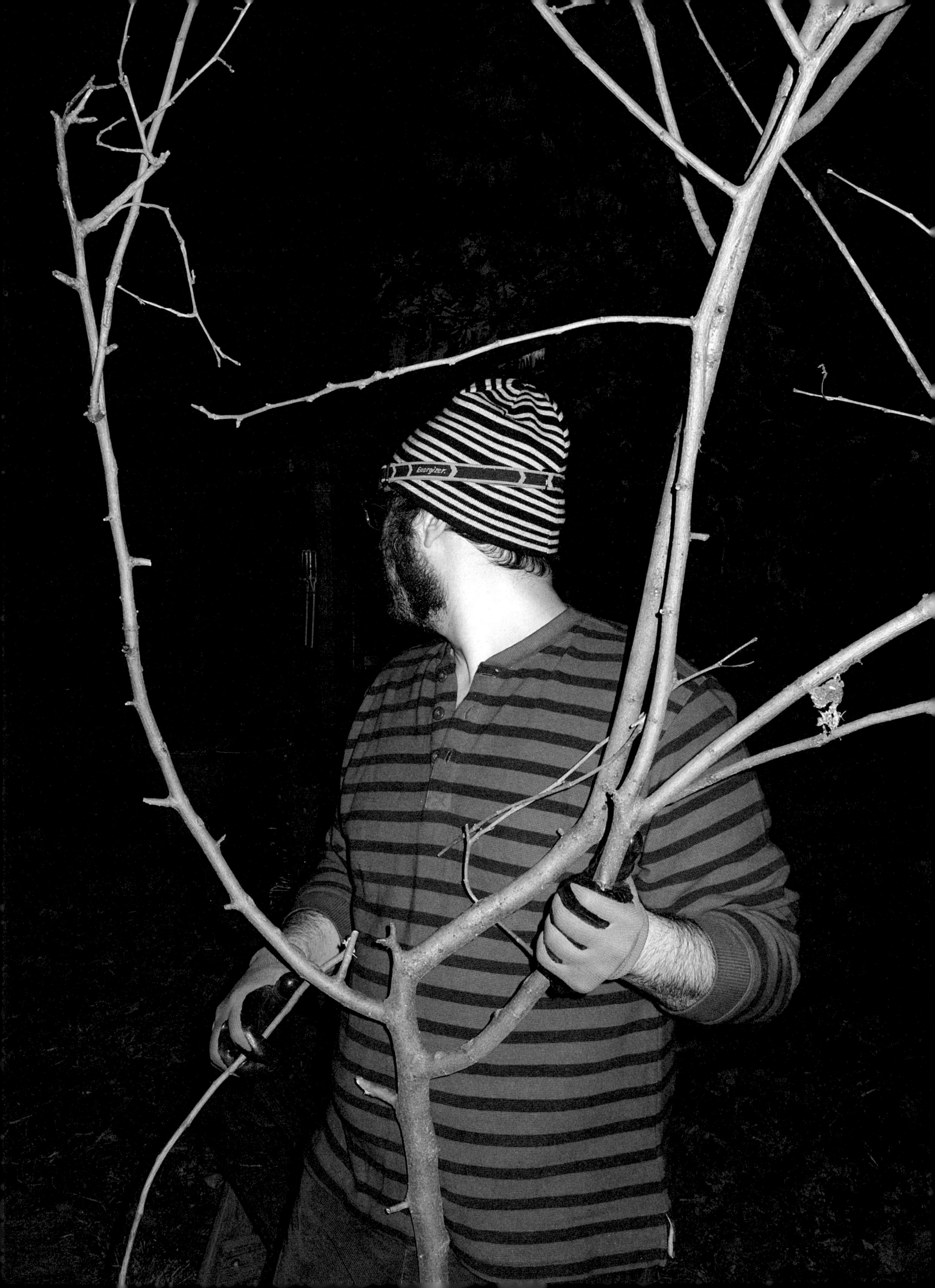
Energizer.

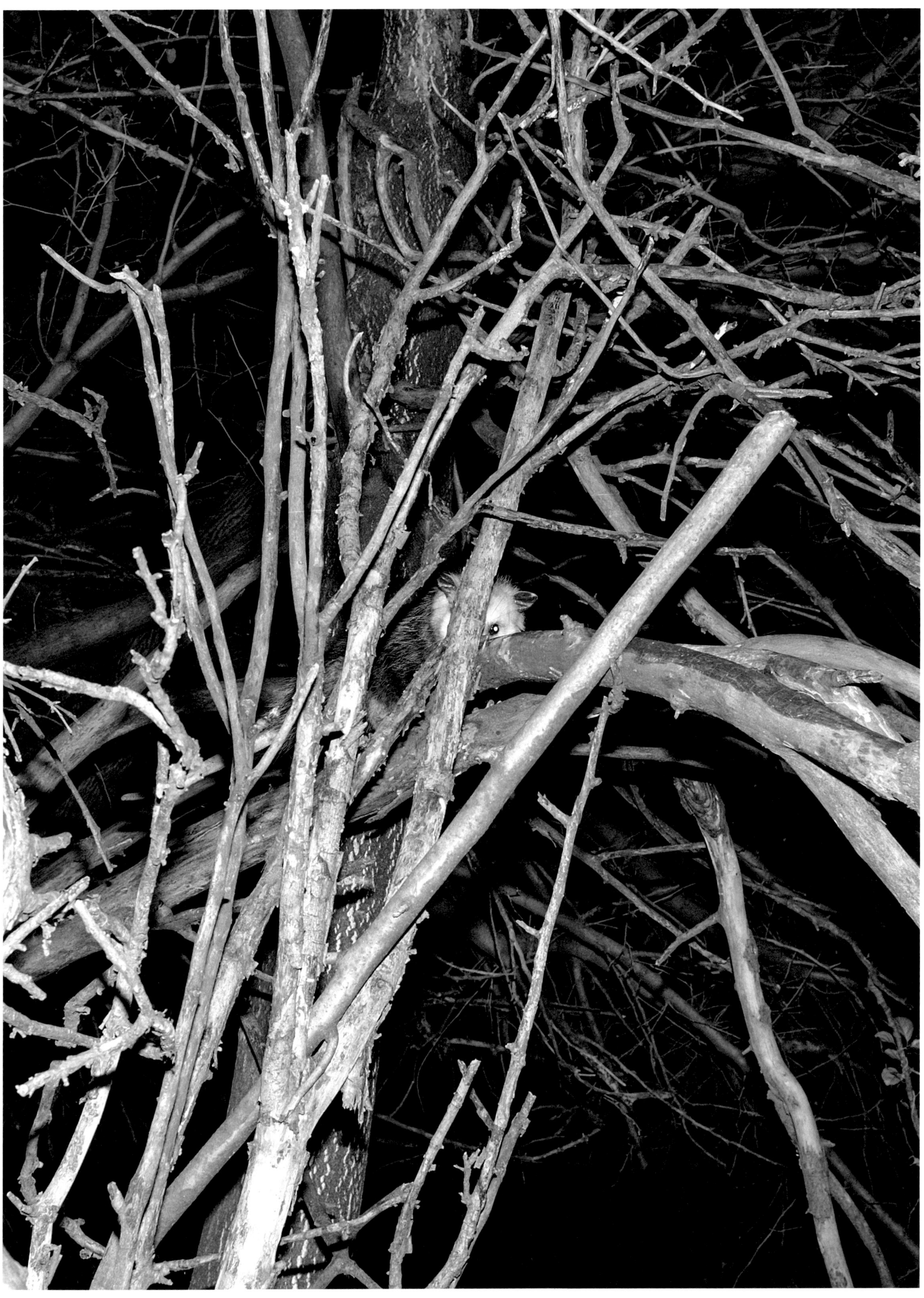

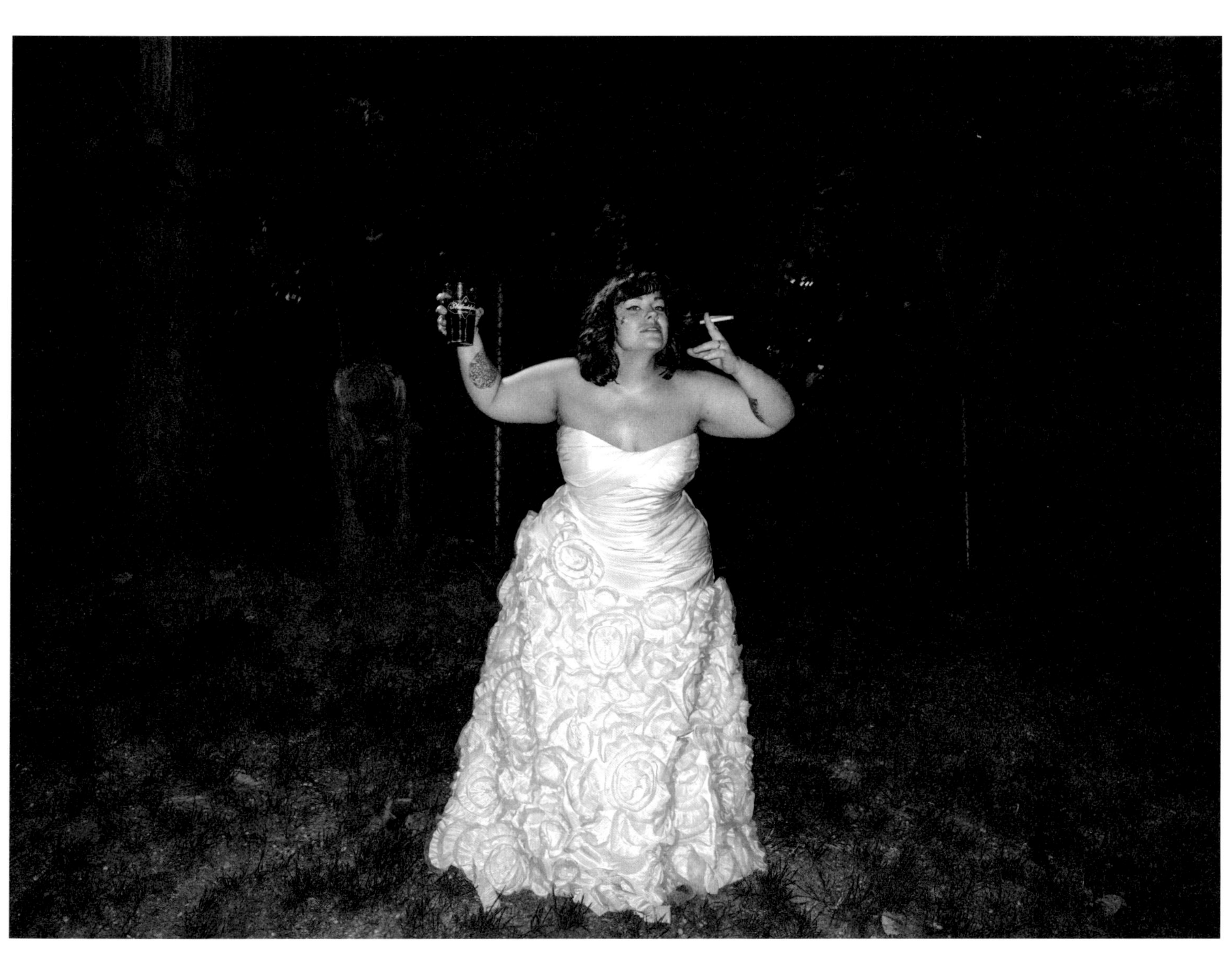

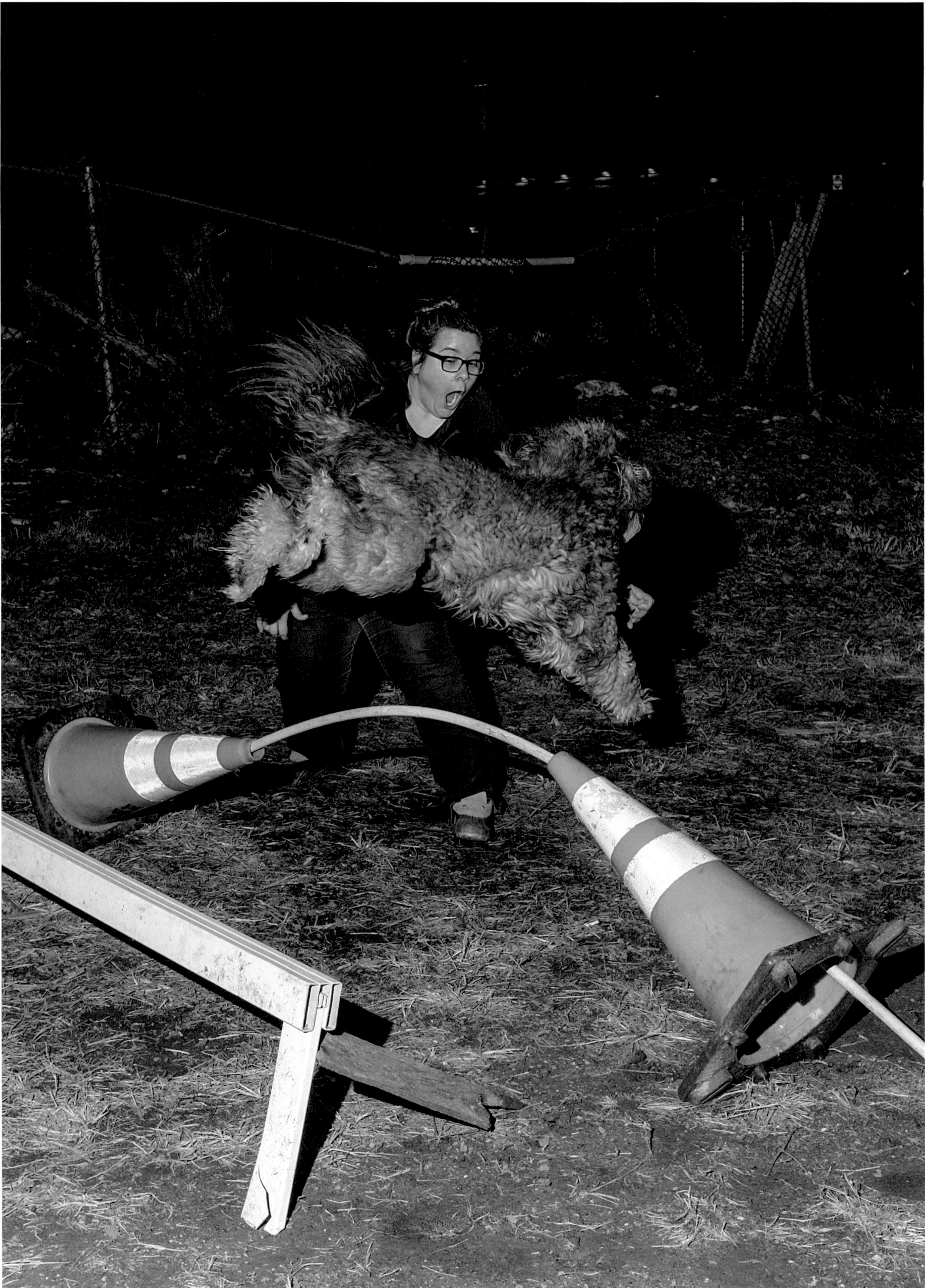

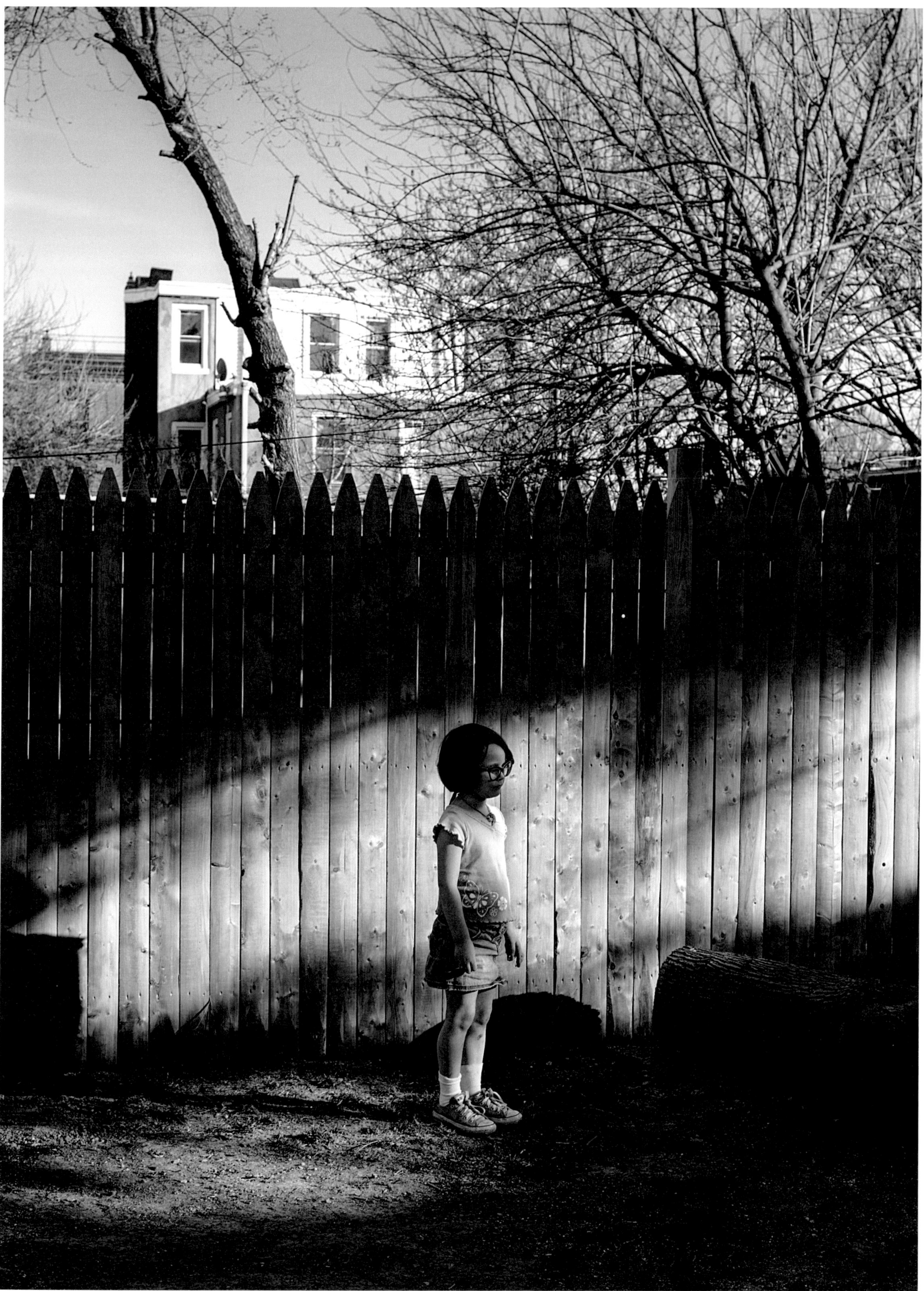

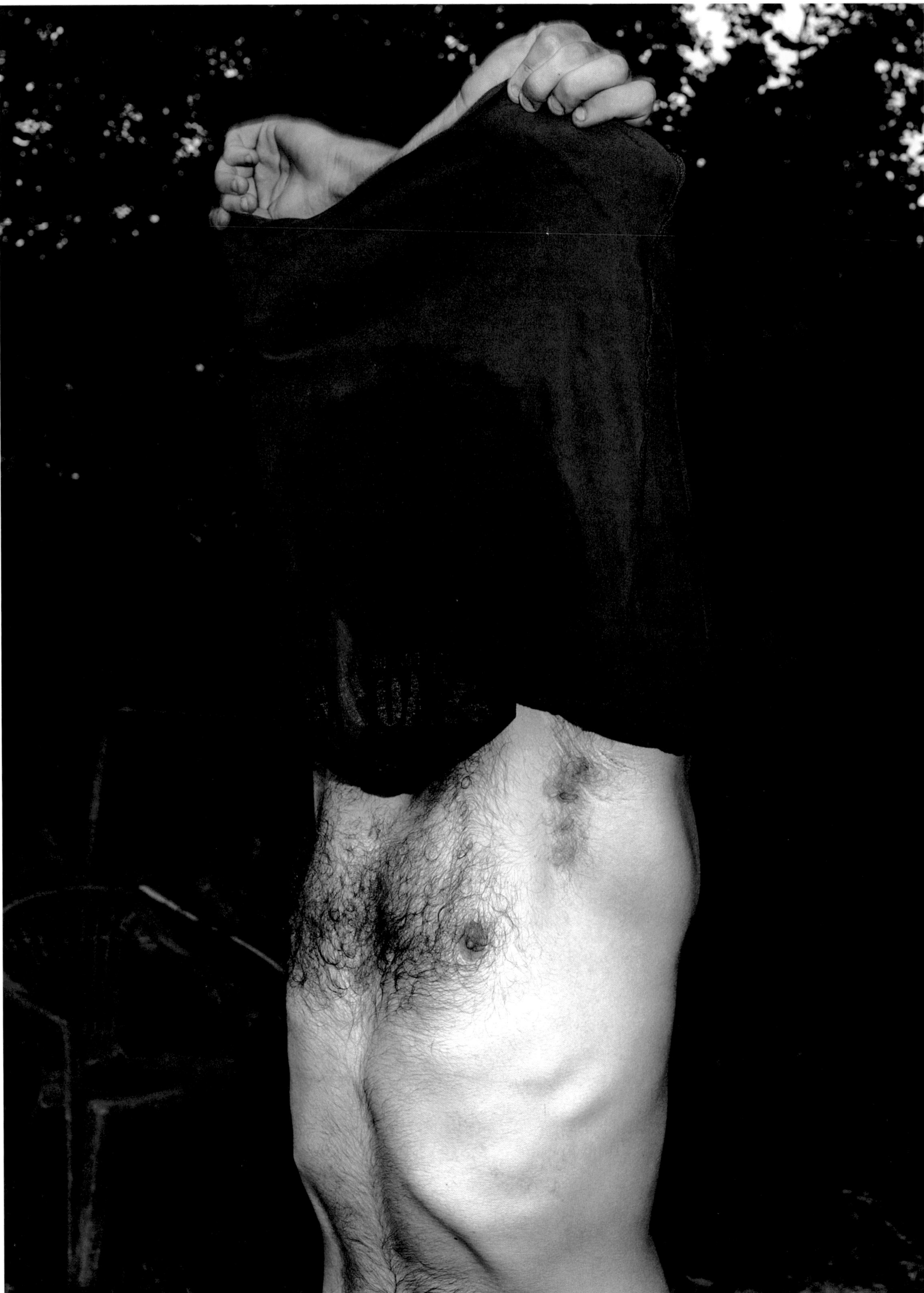

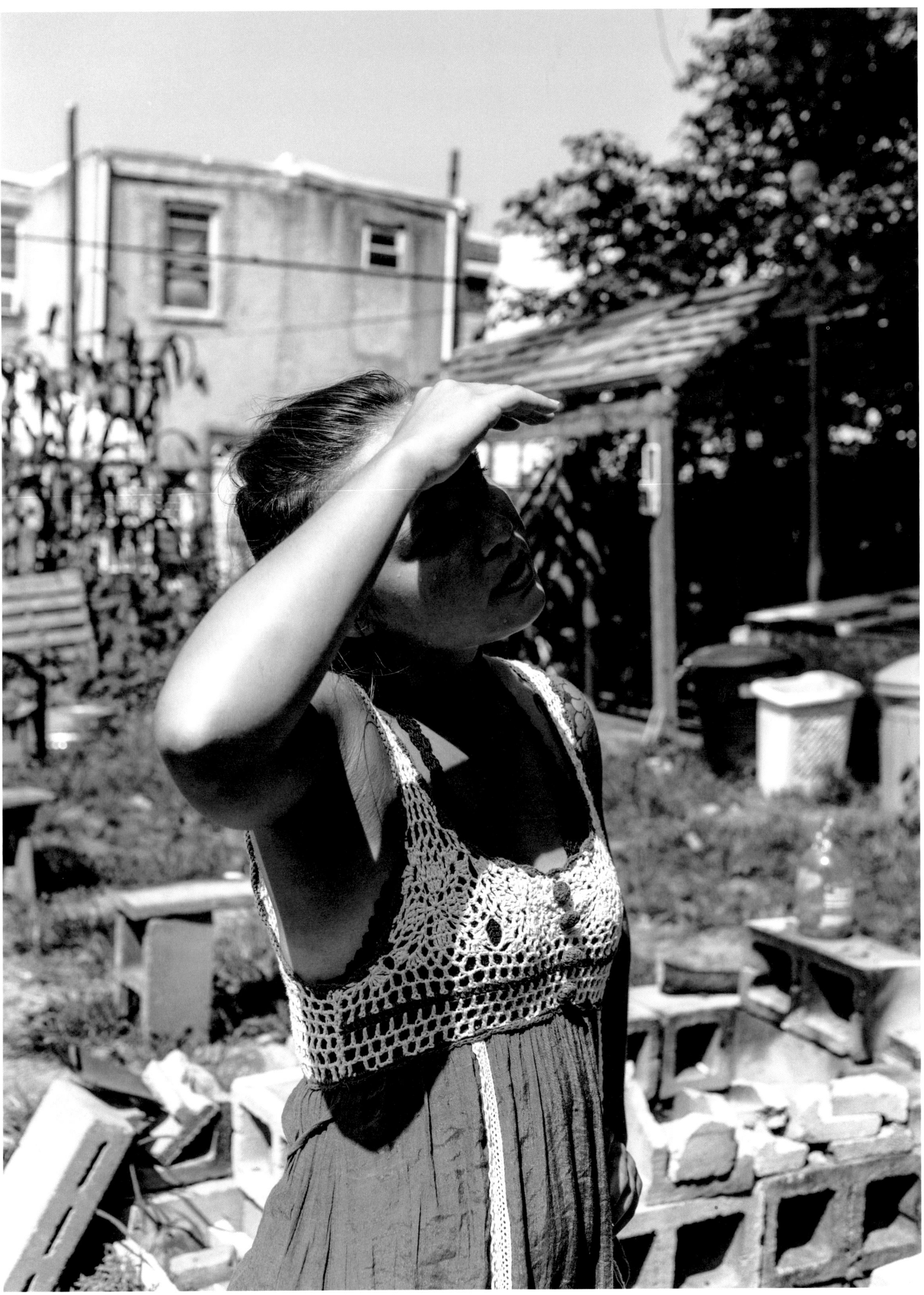

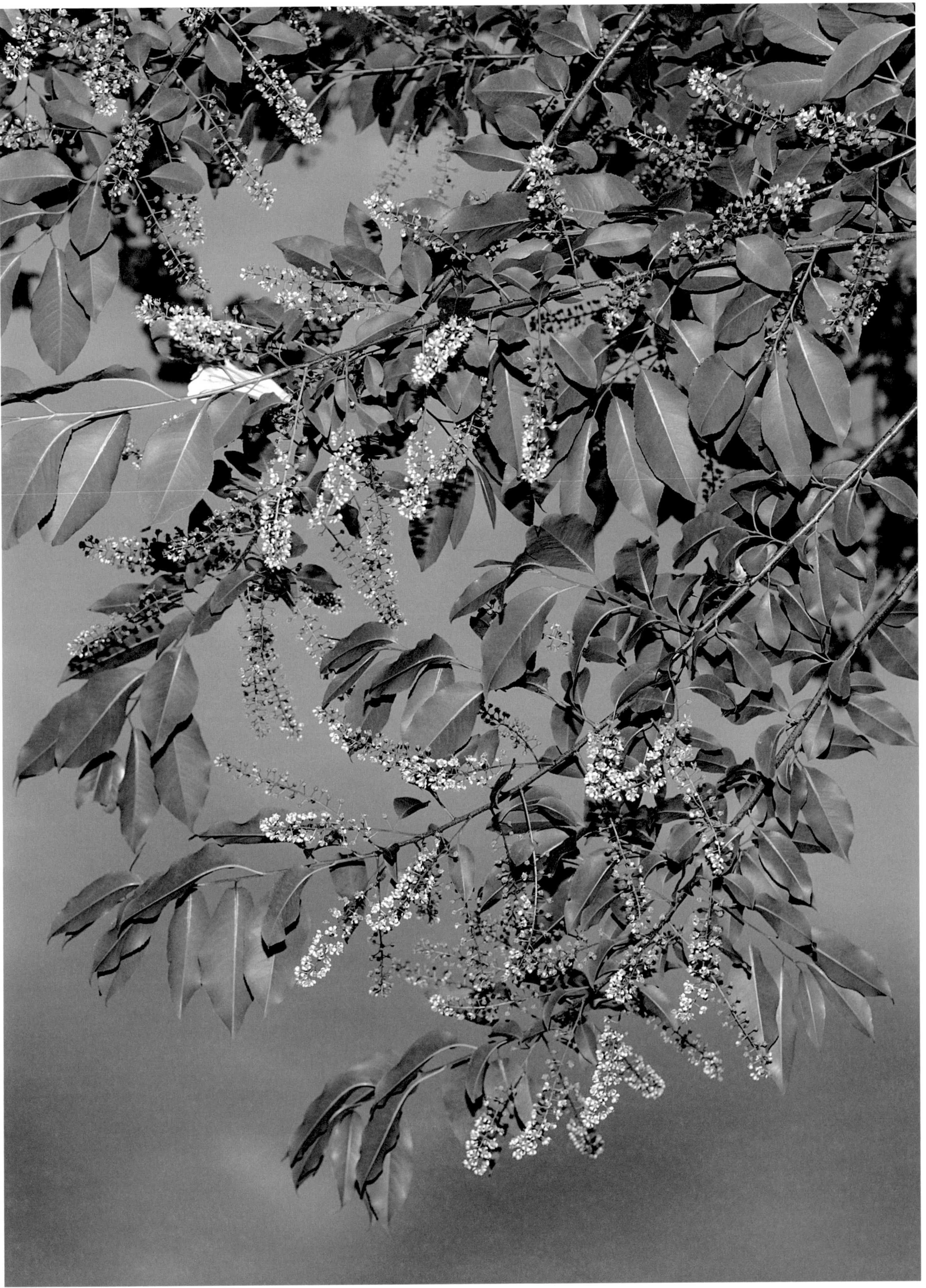

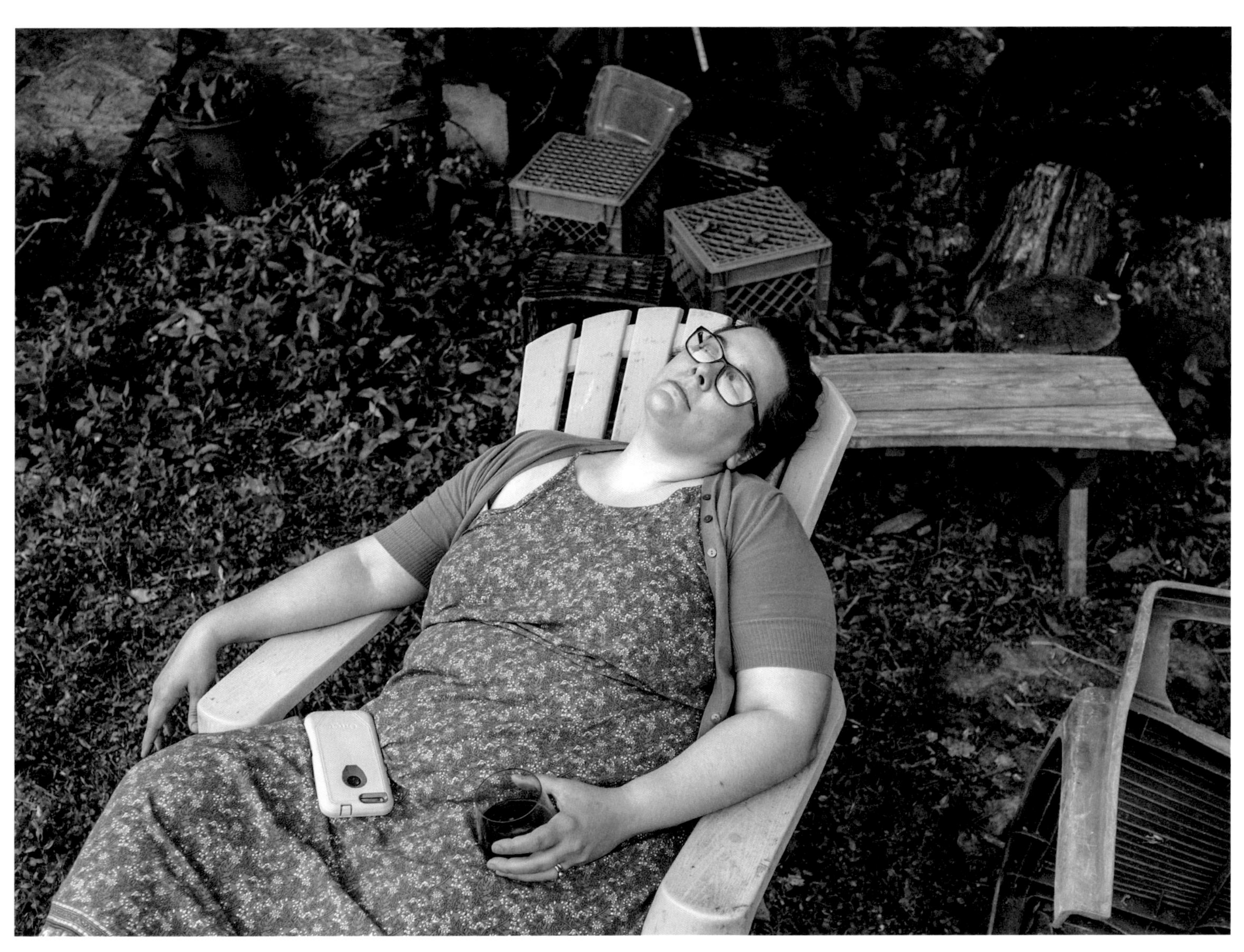

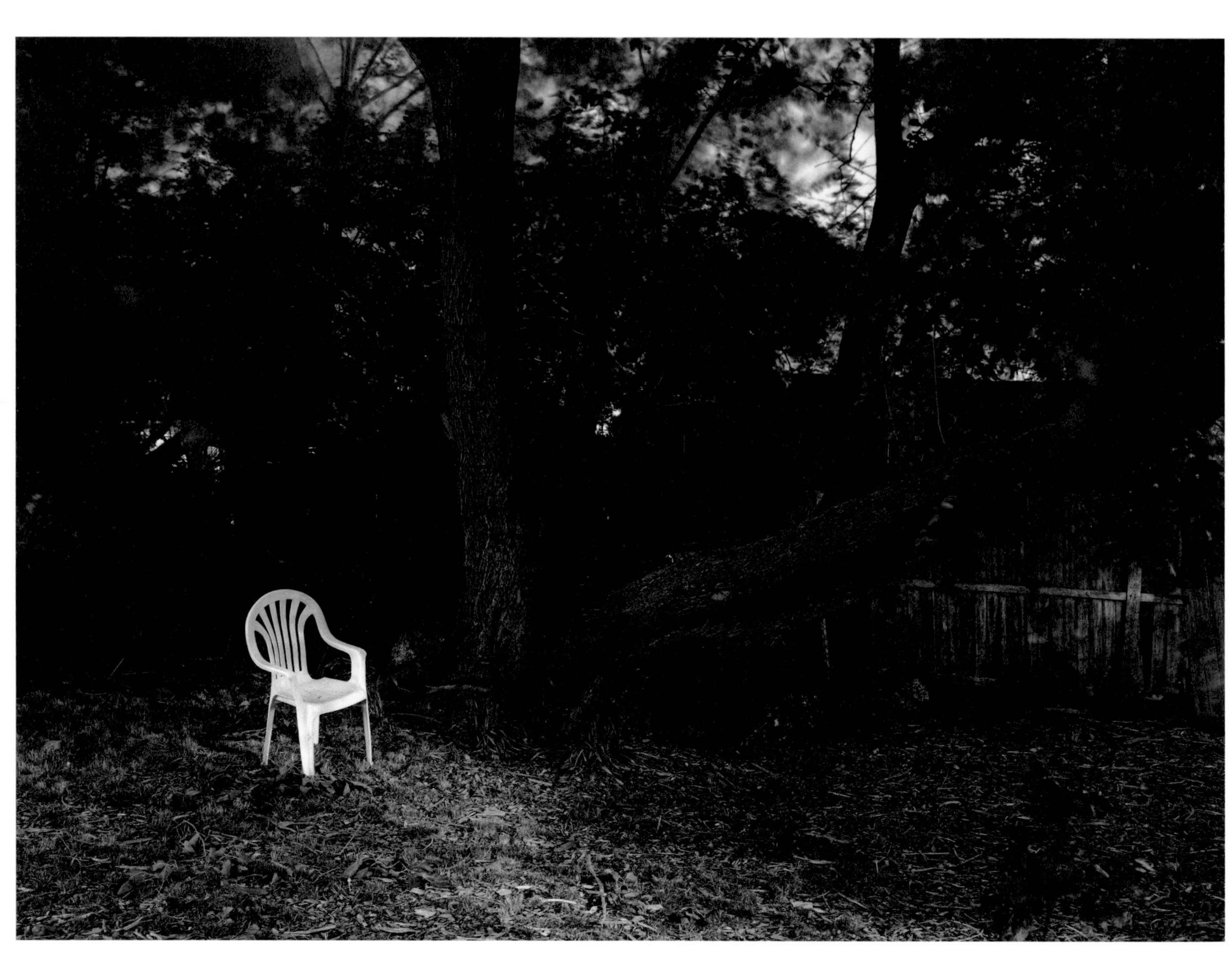

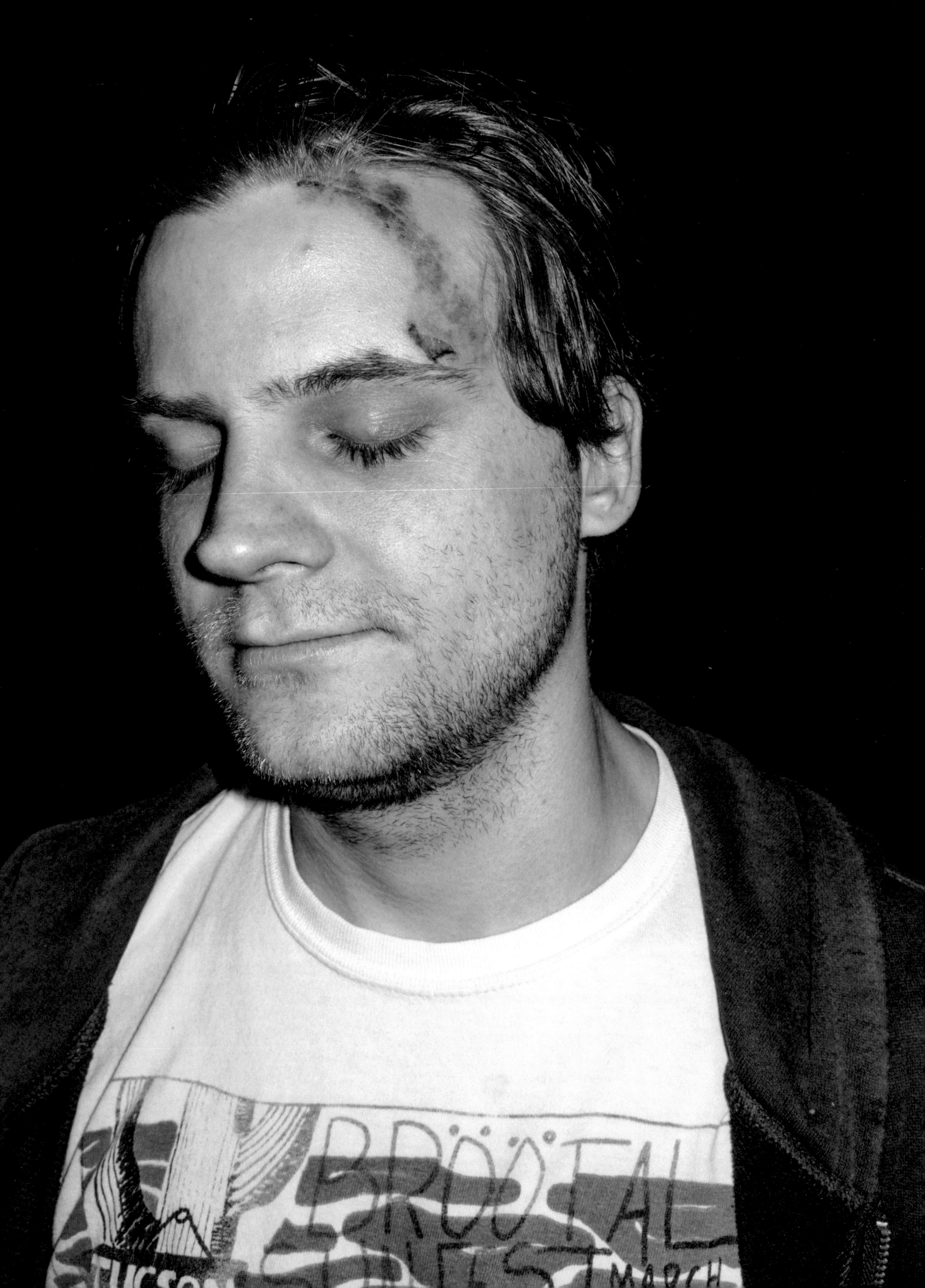
BRÖÖTAL

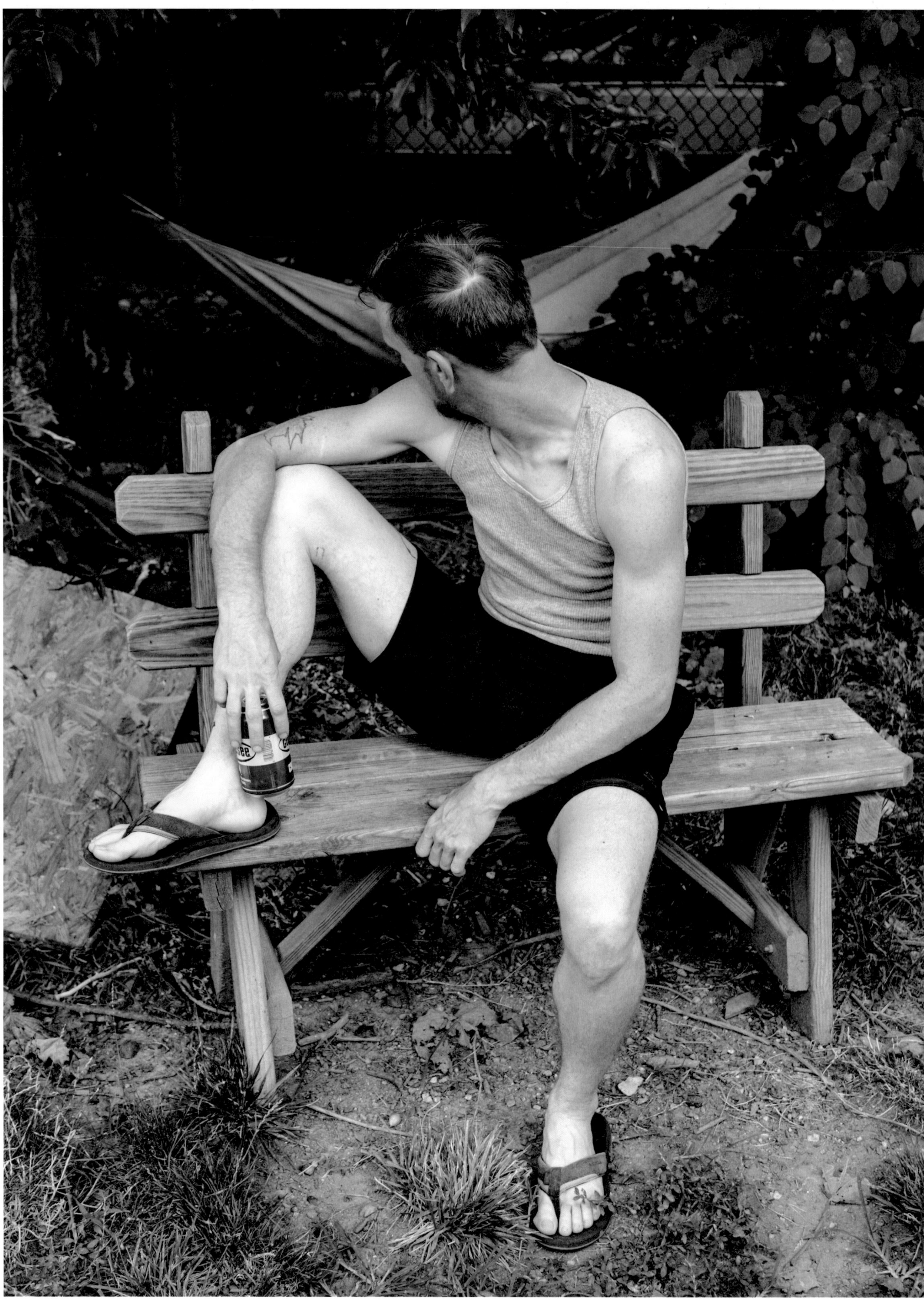

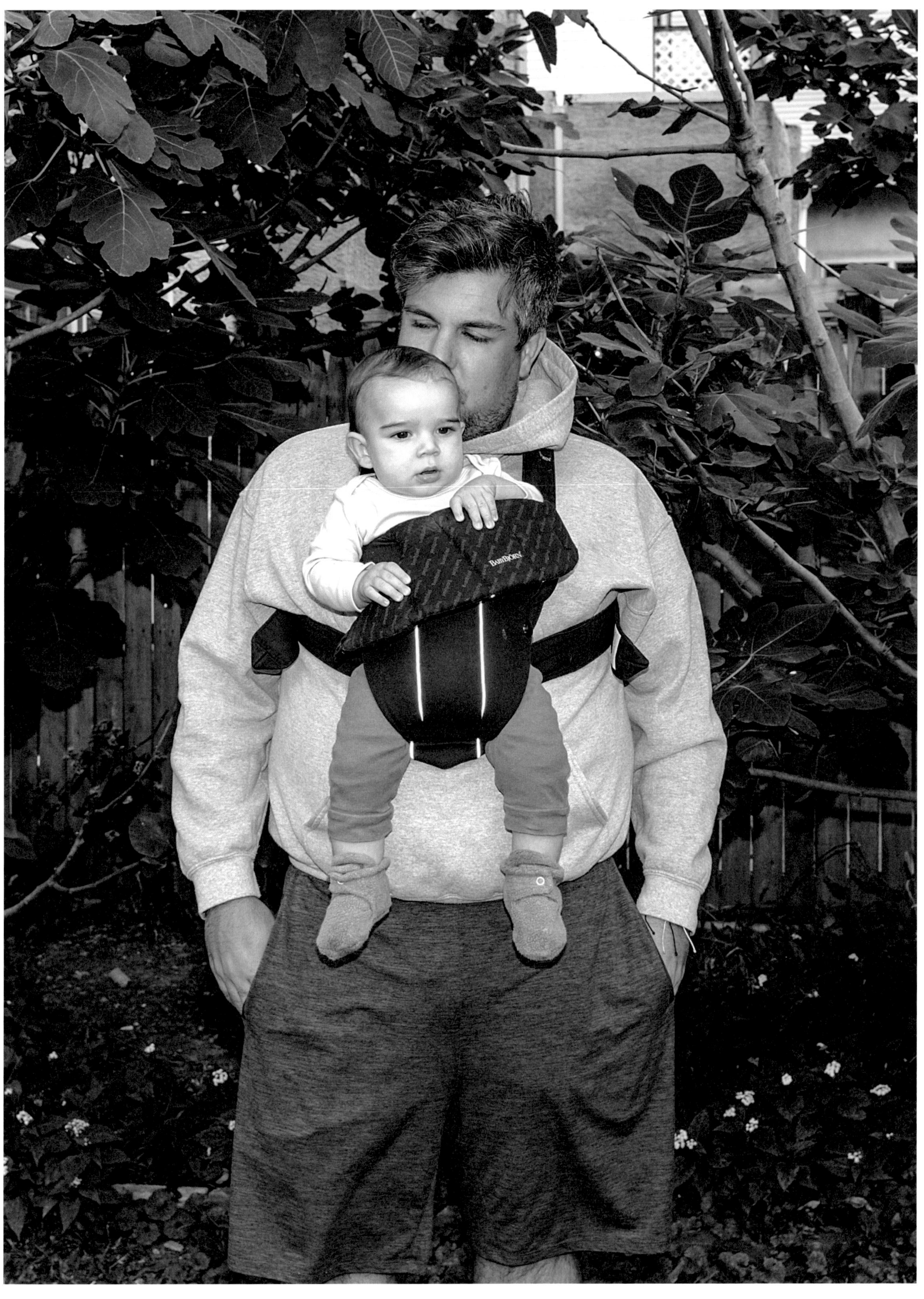
BABYBJÖRN

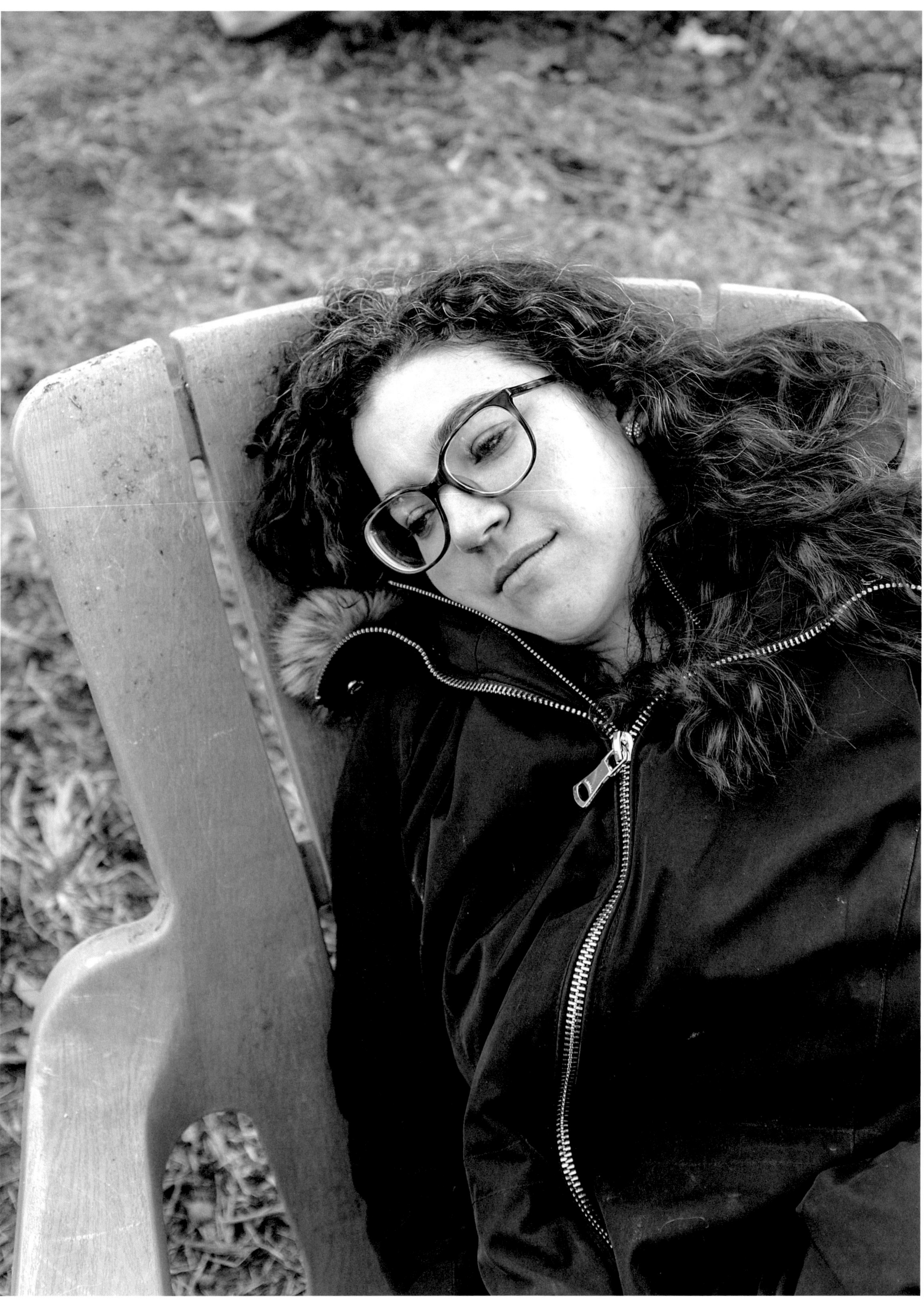

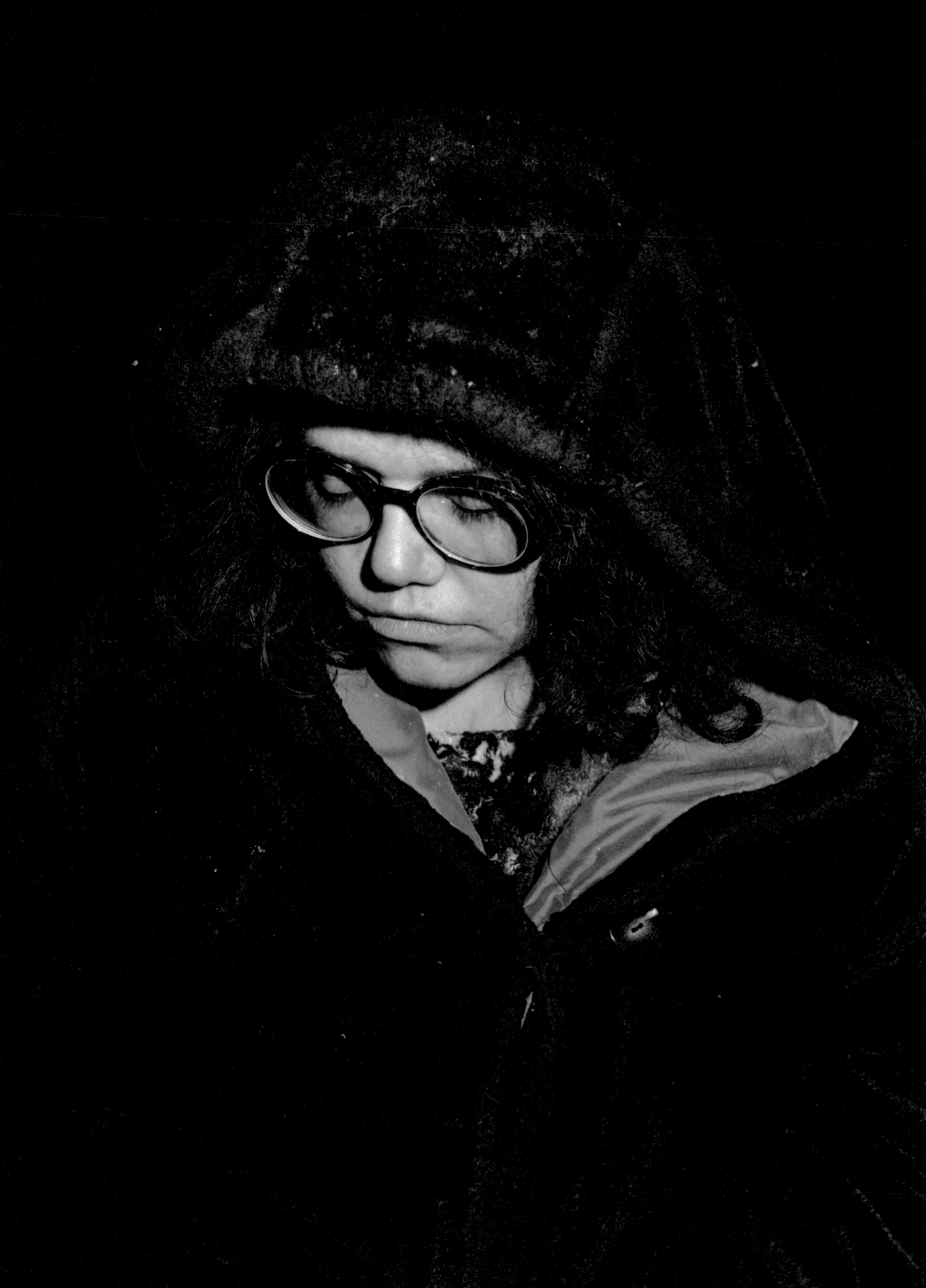

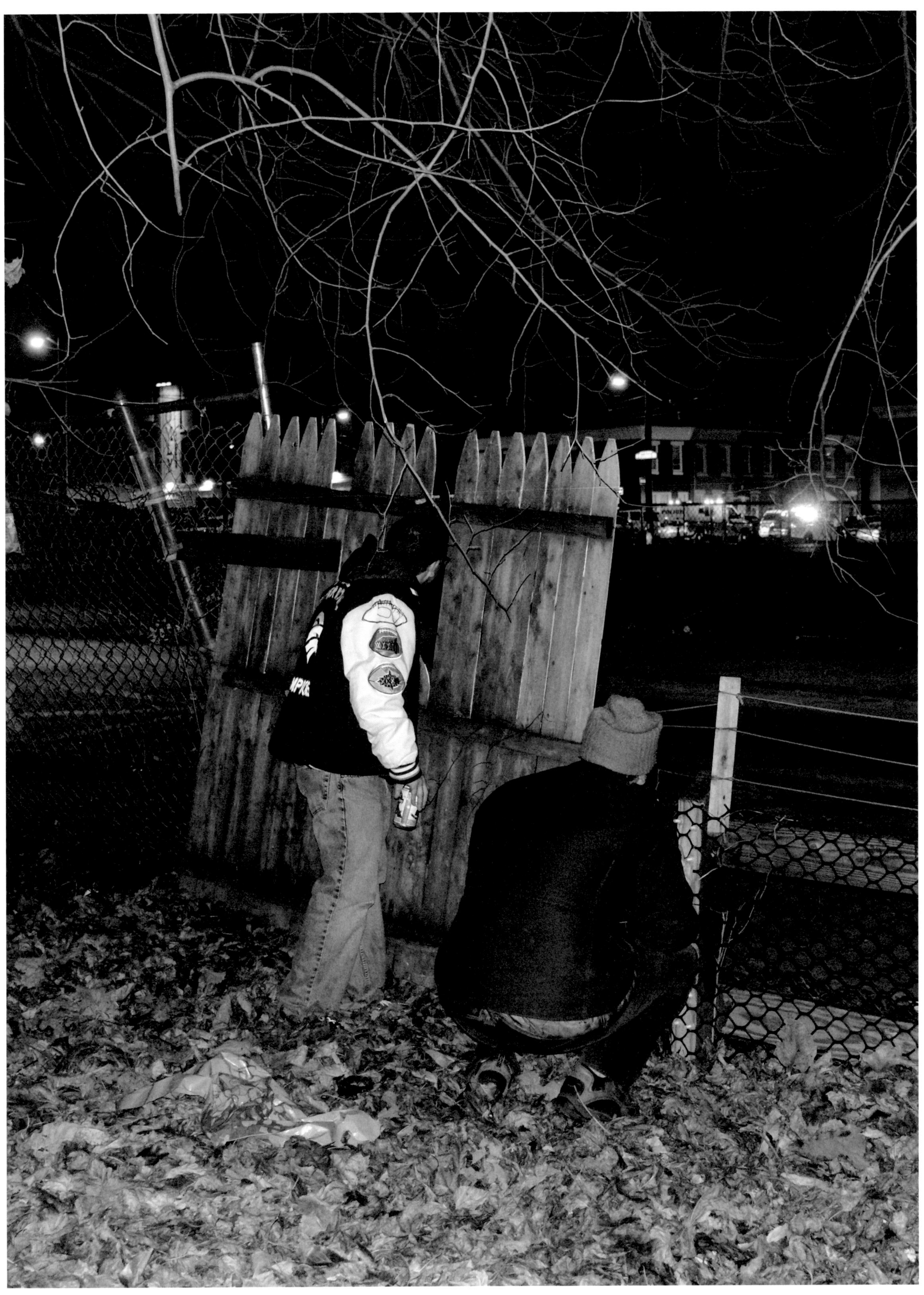

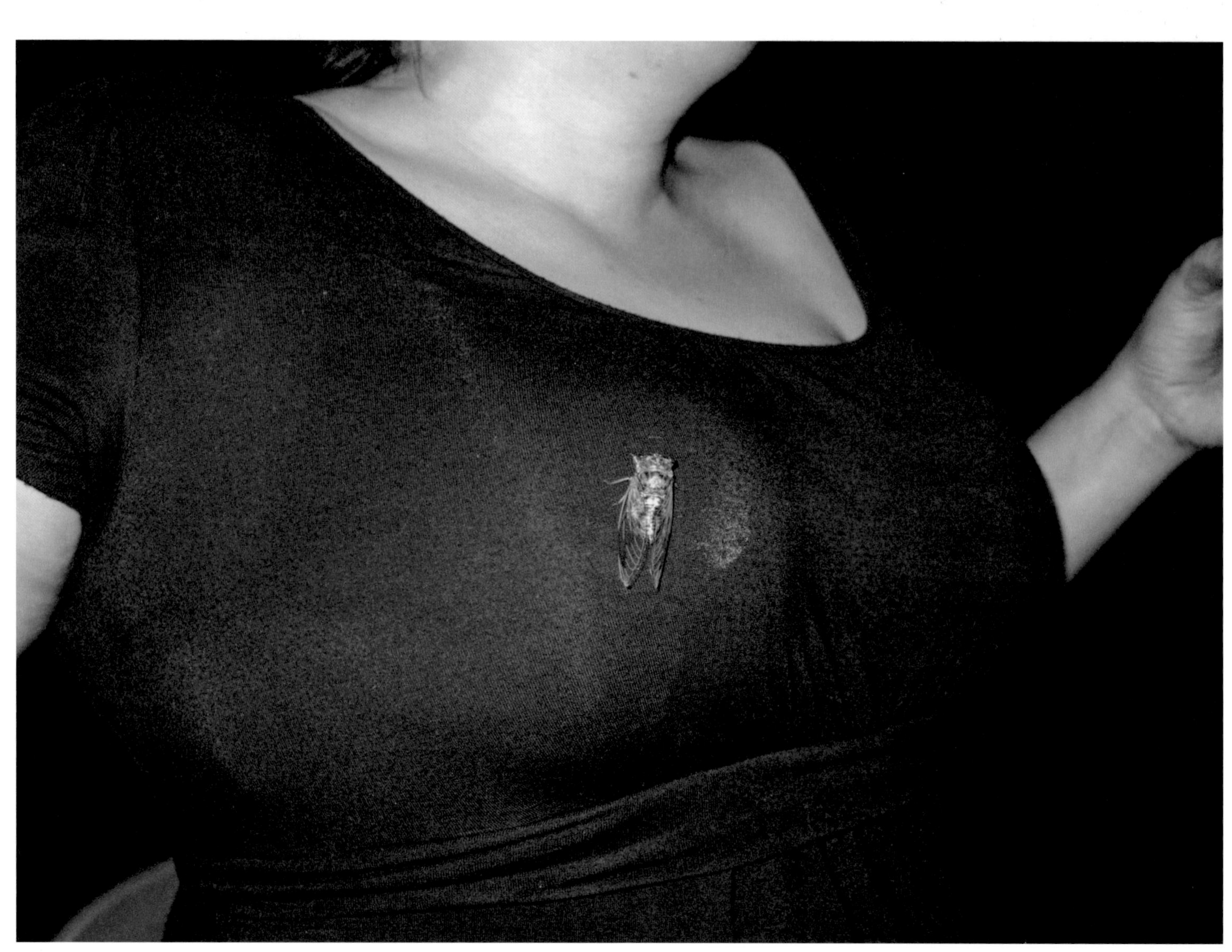

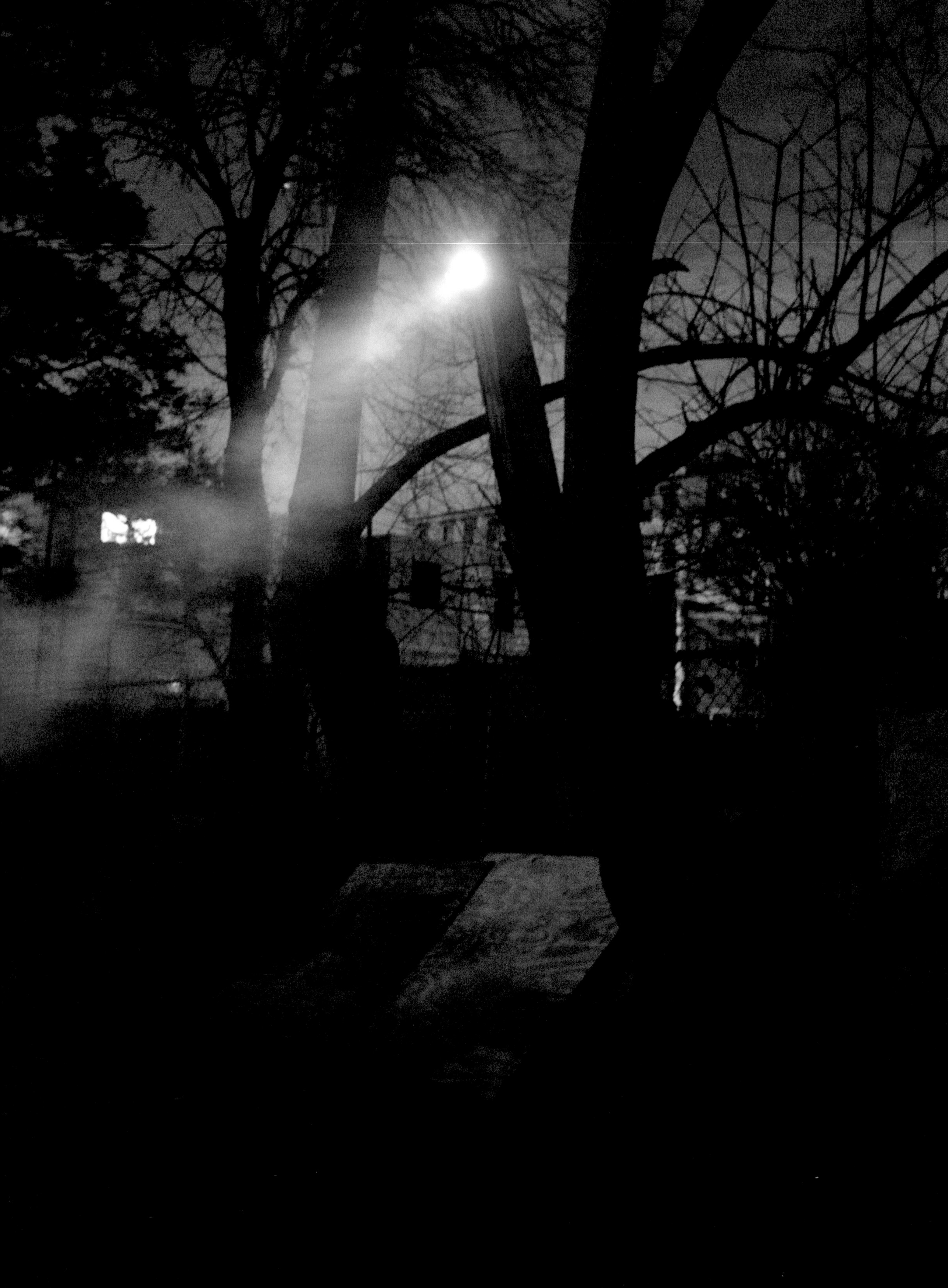

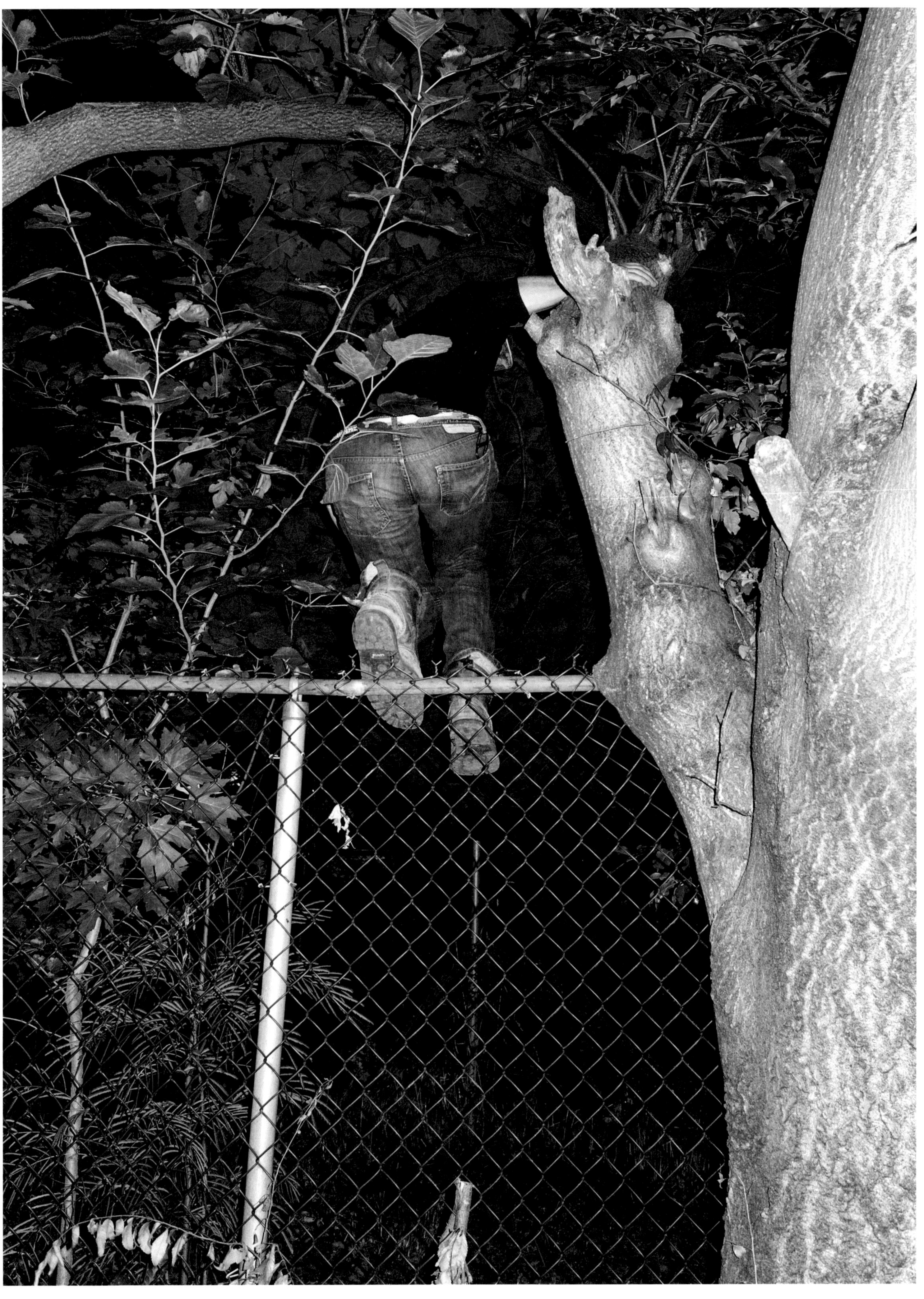

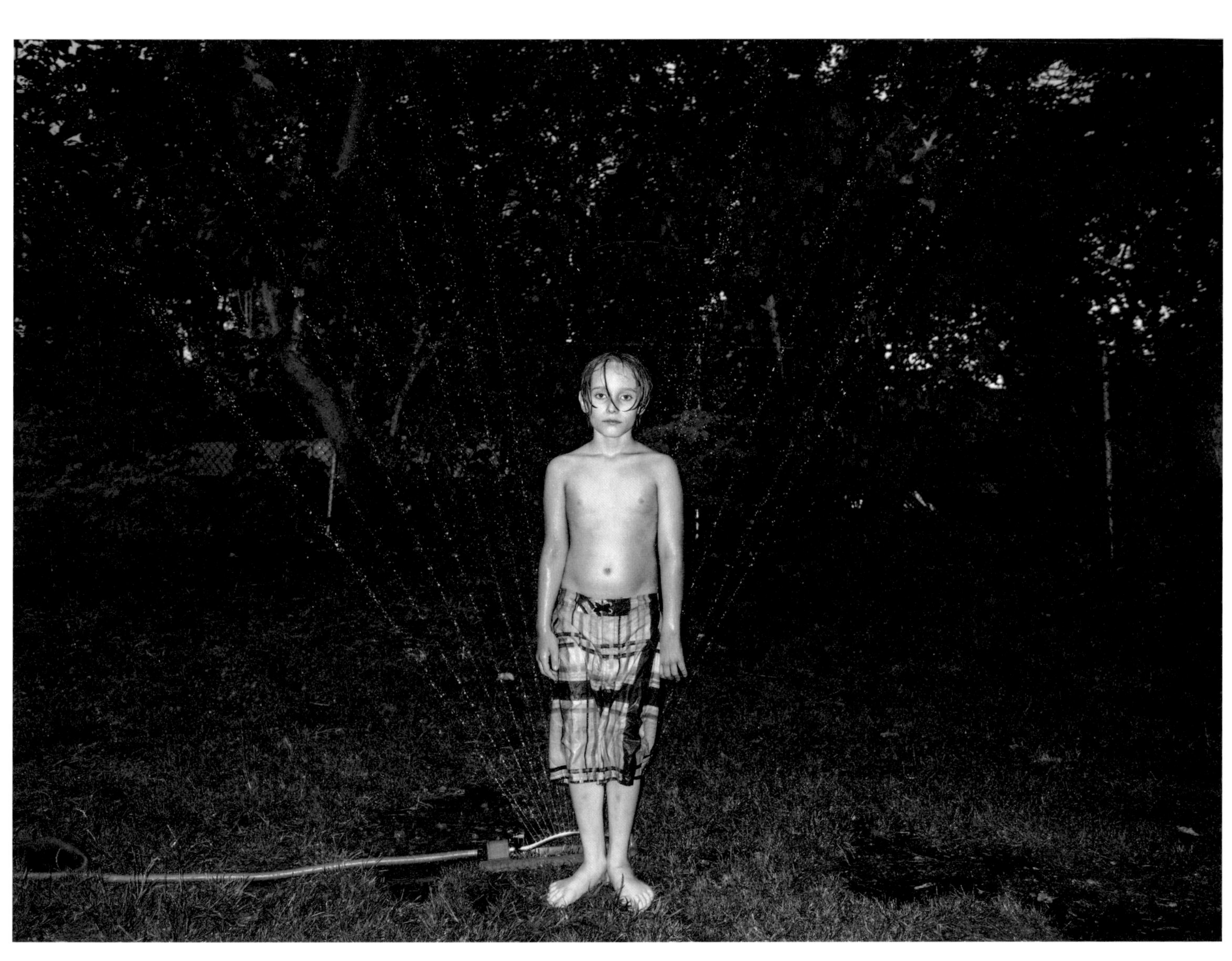

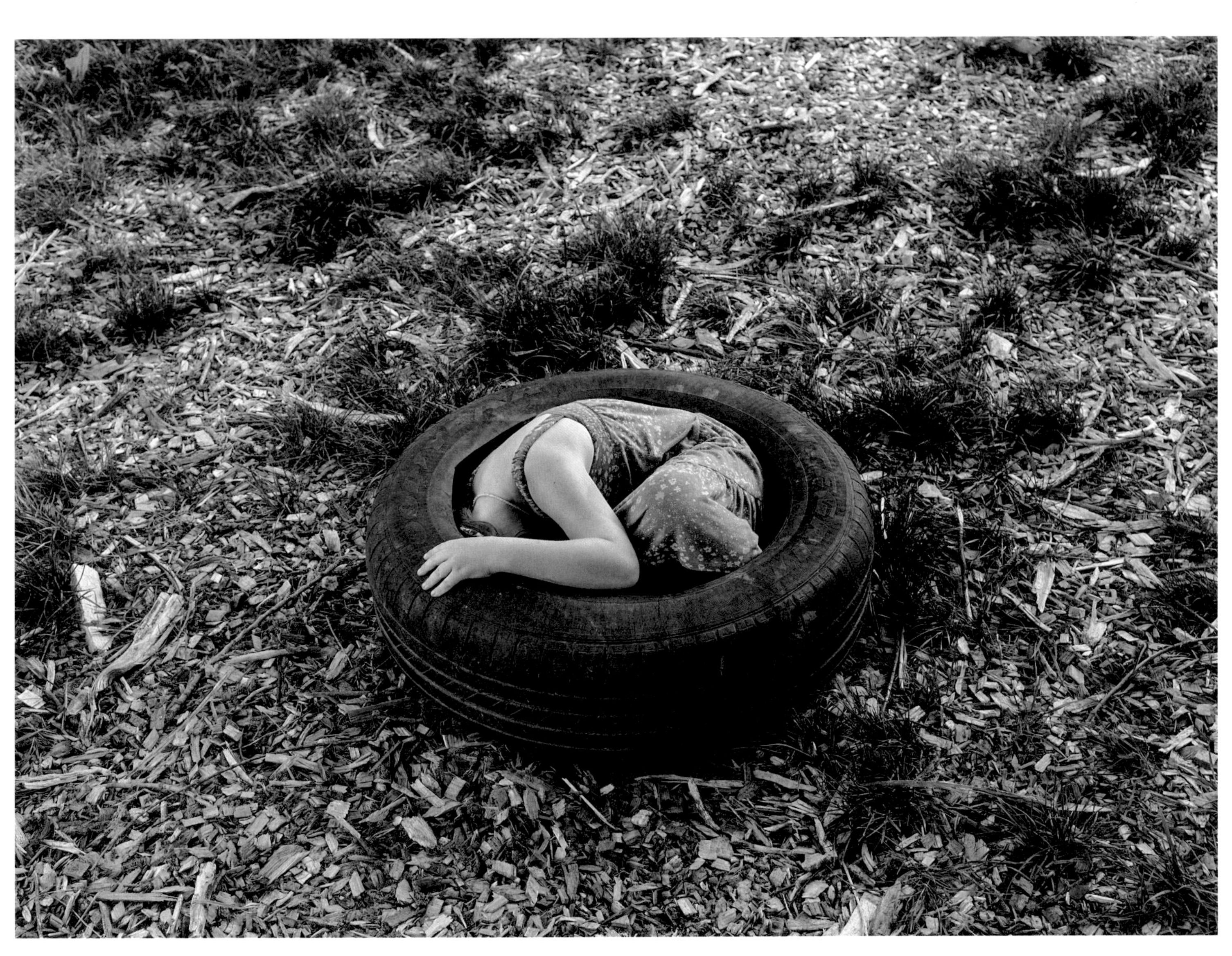

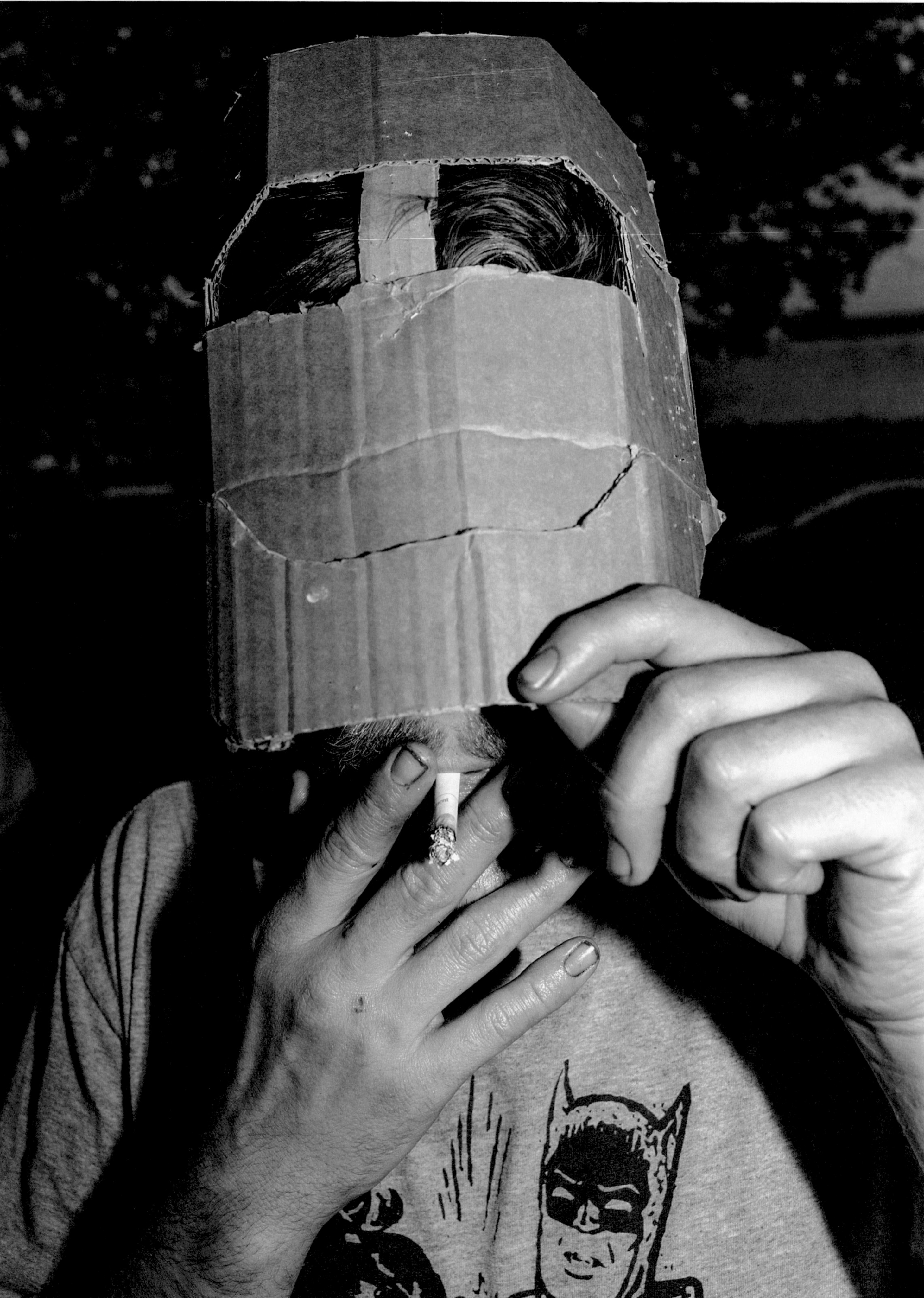

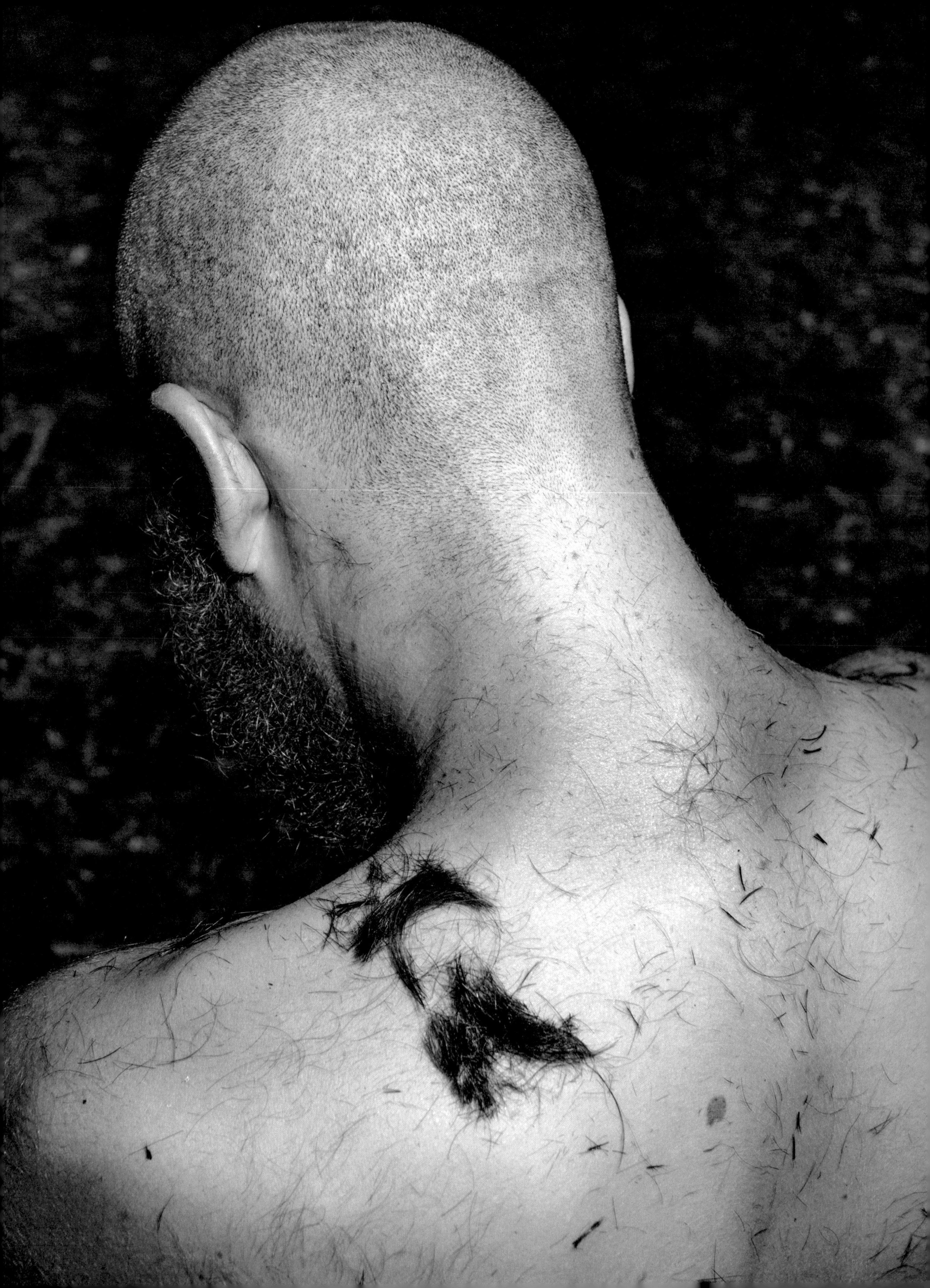

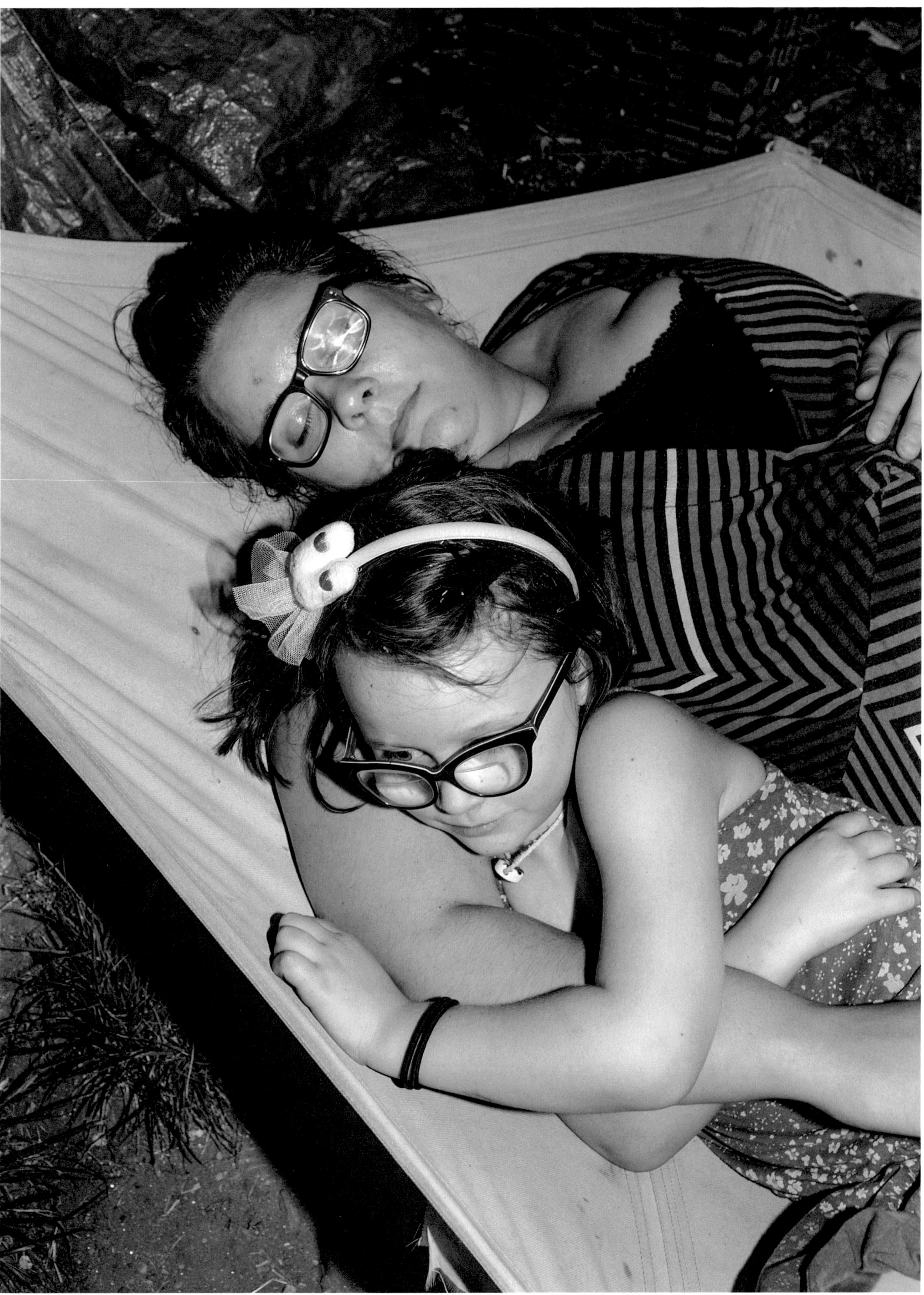

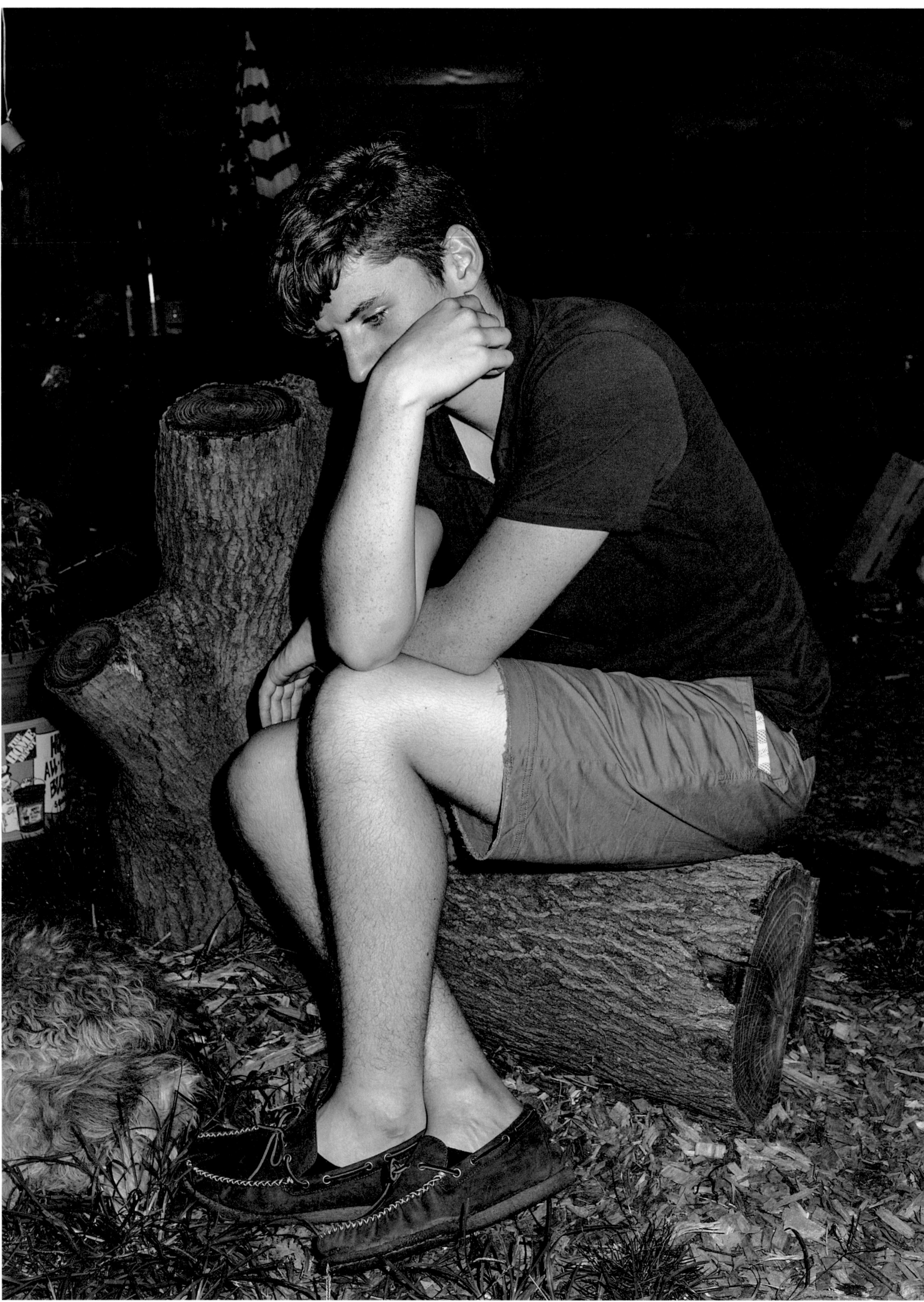

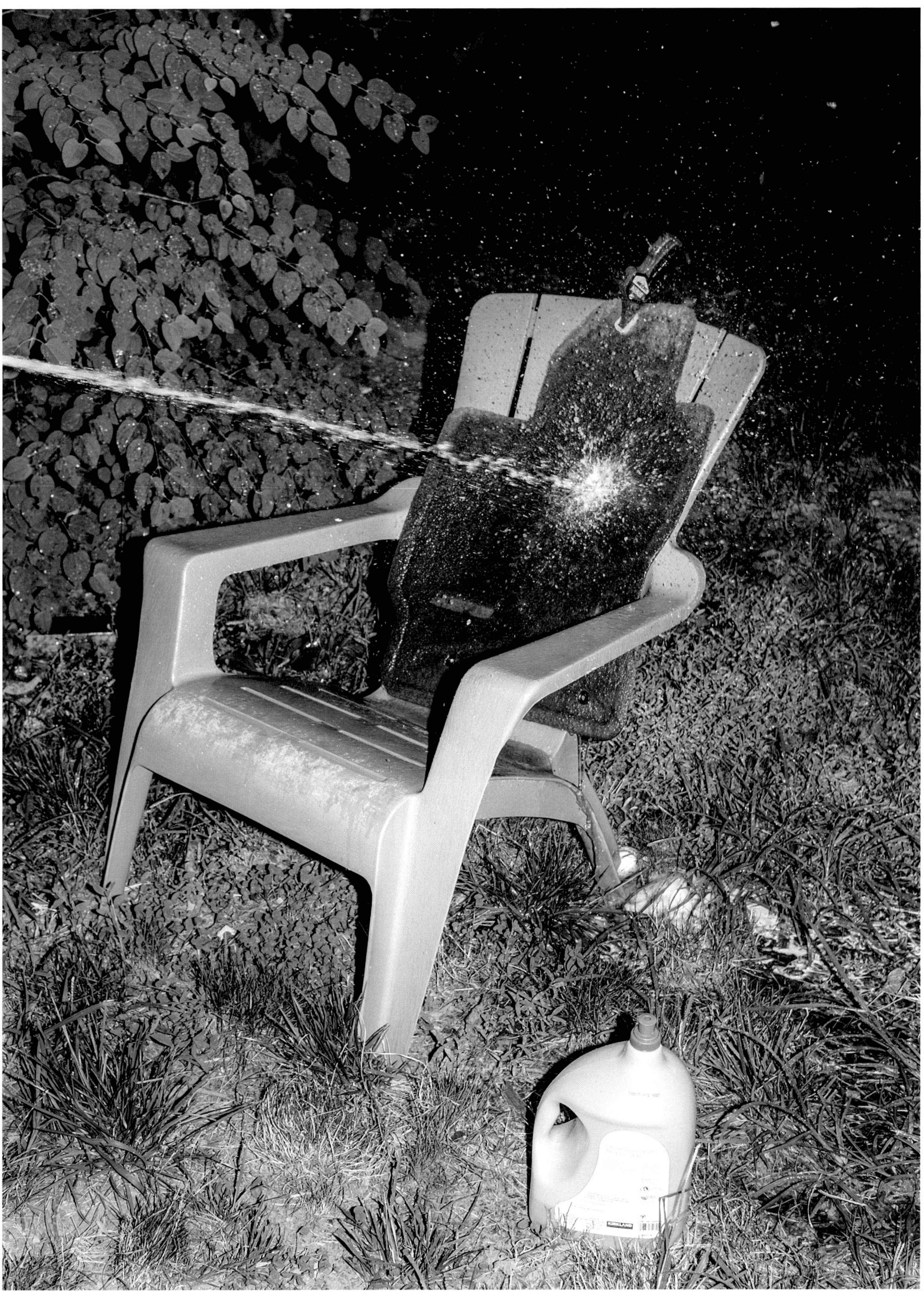

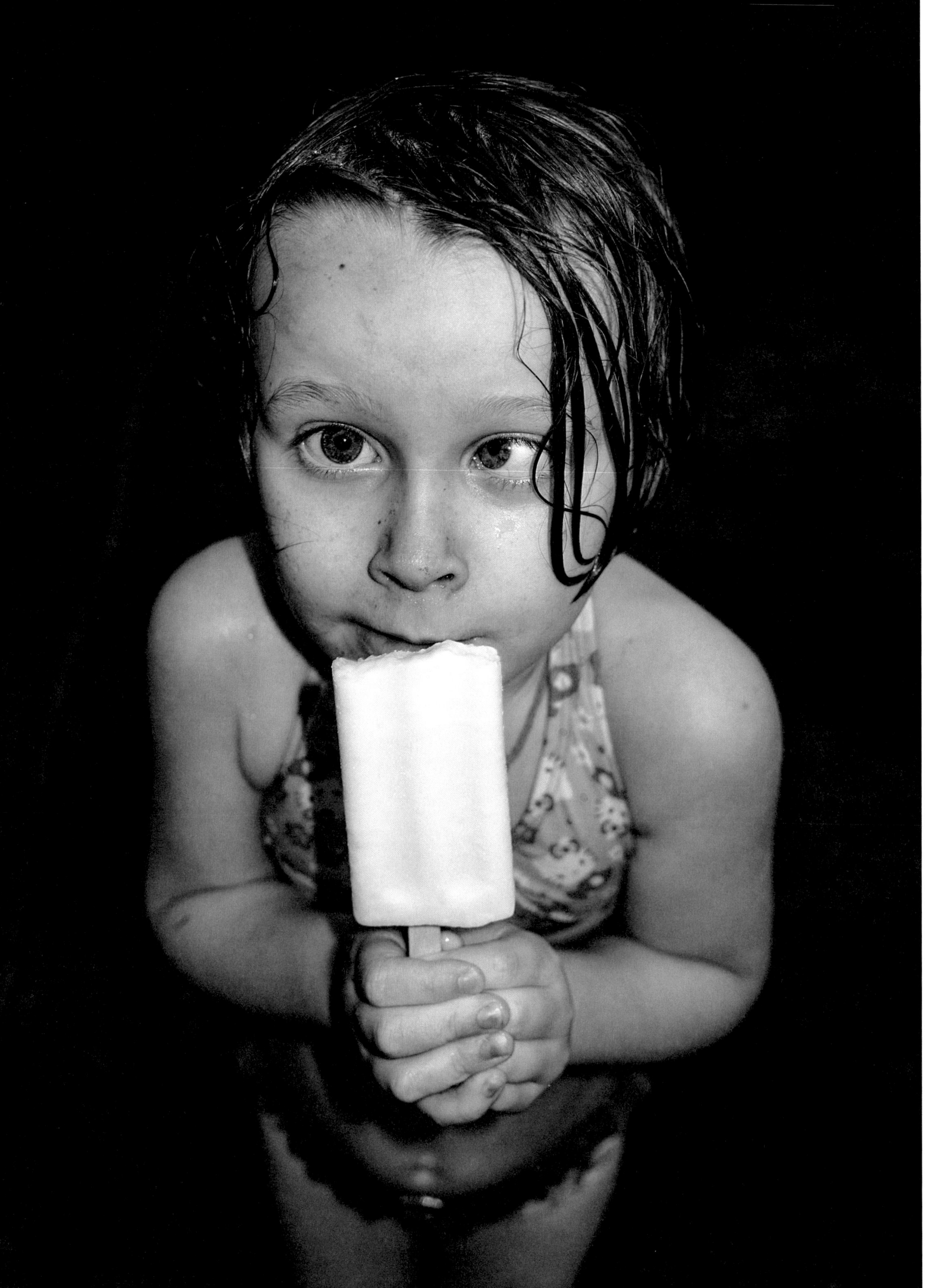

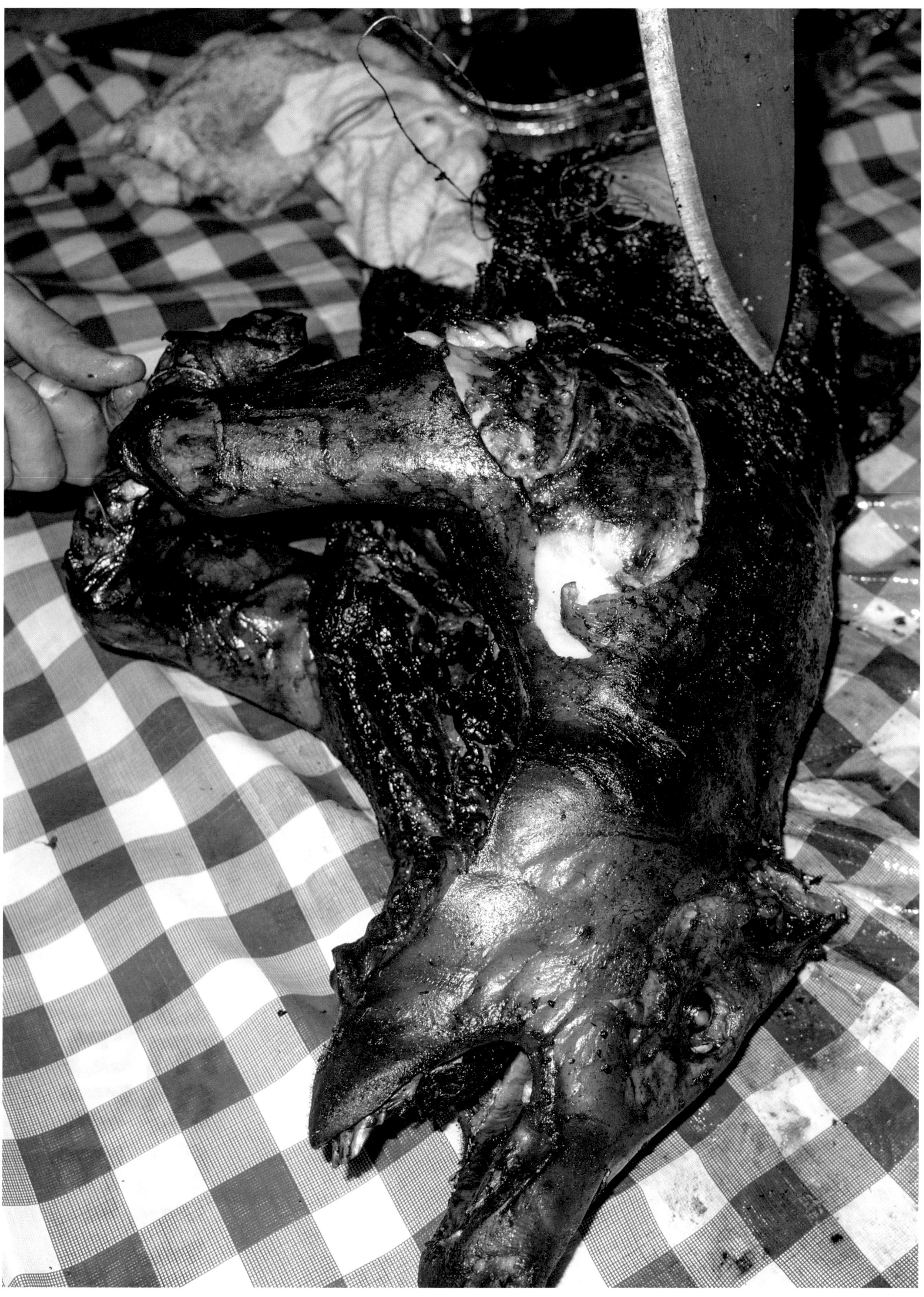

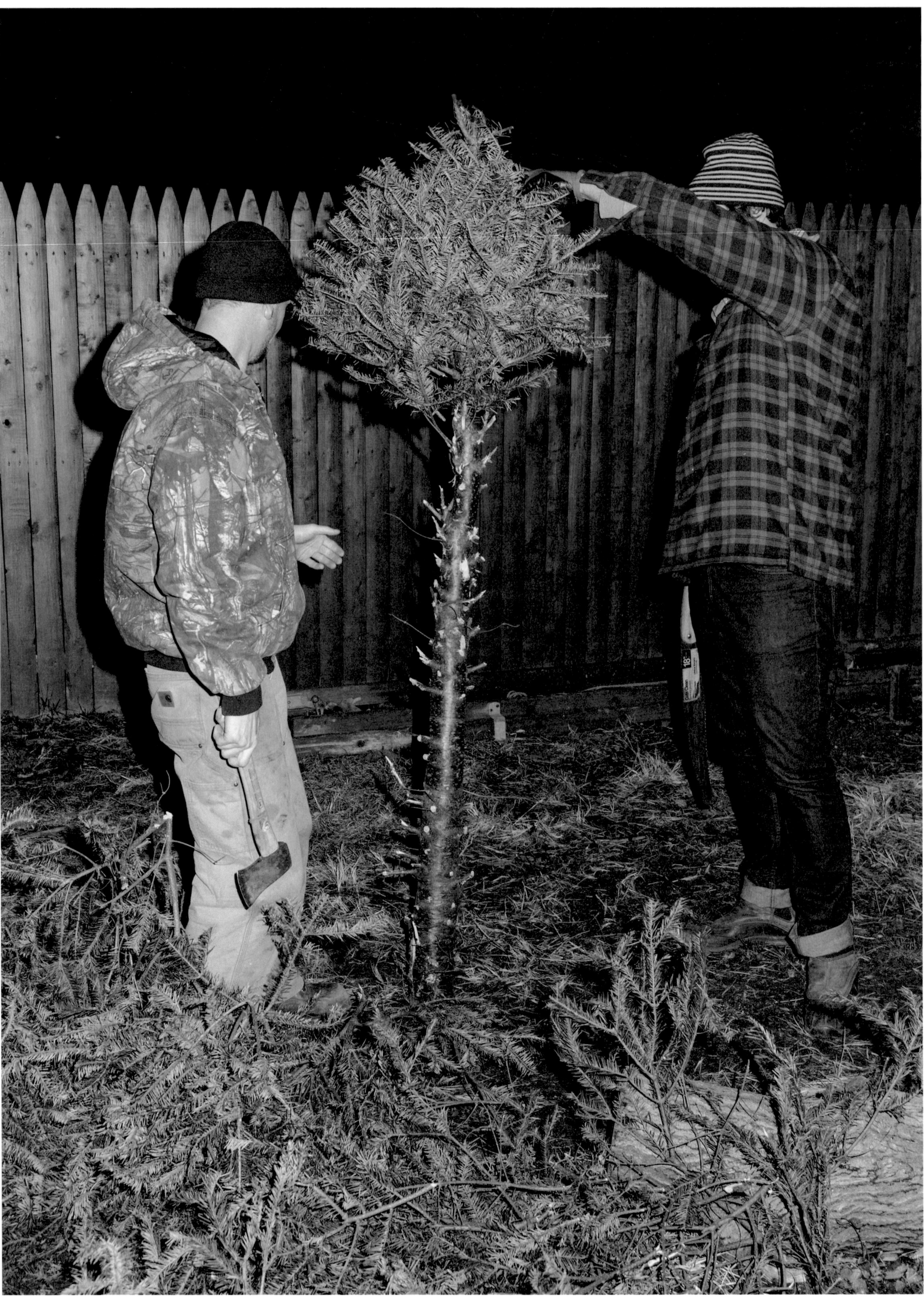

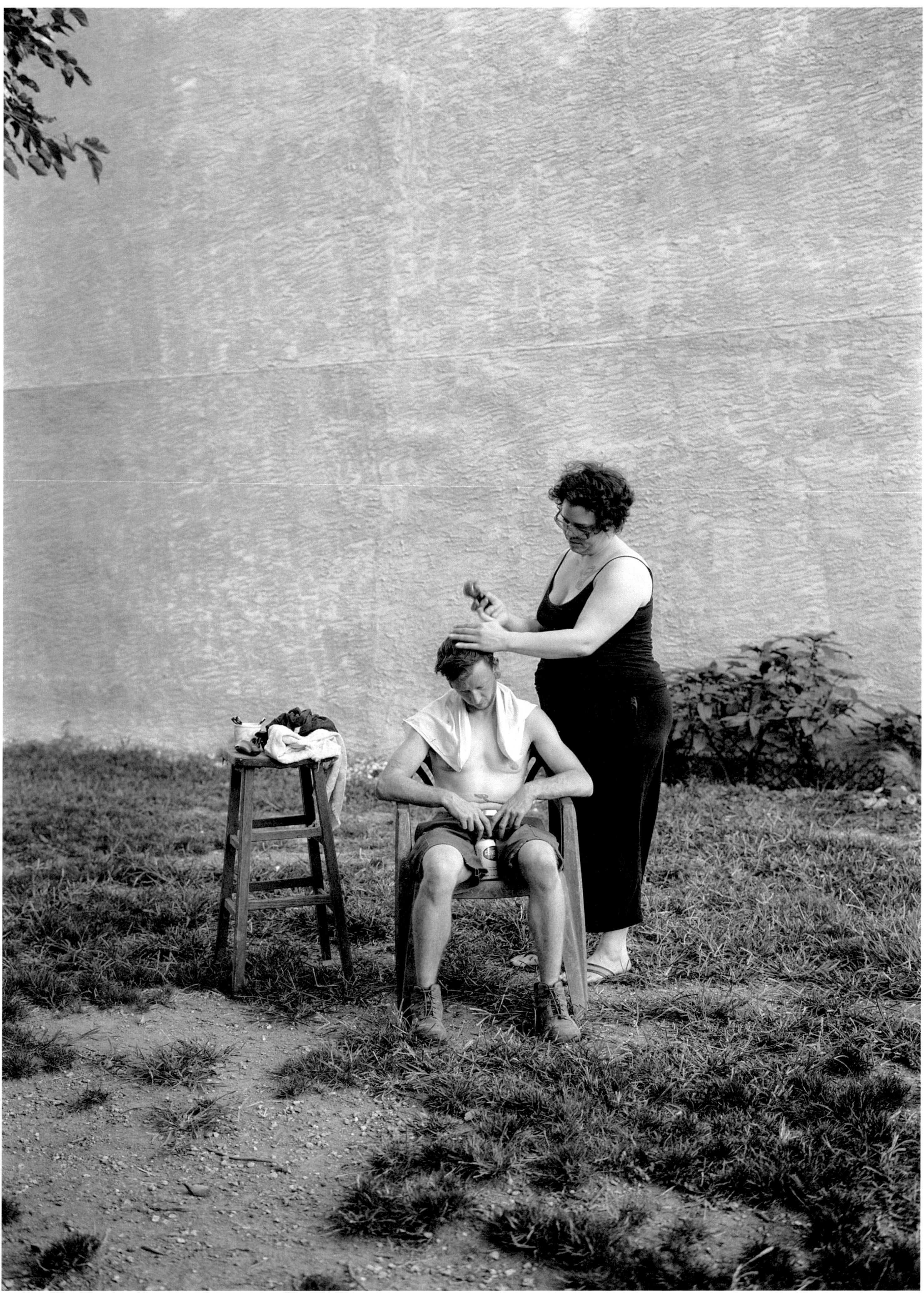

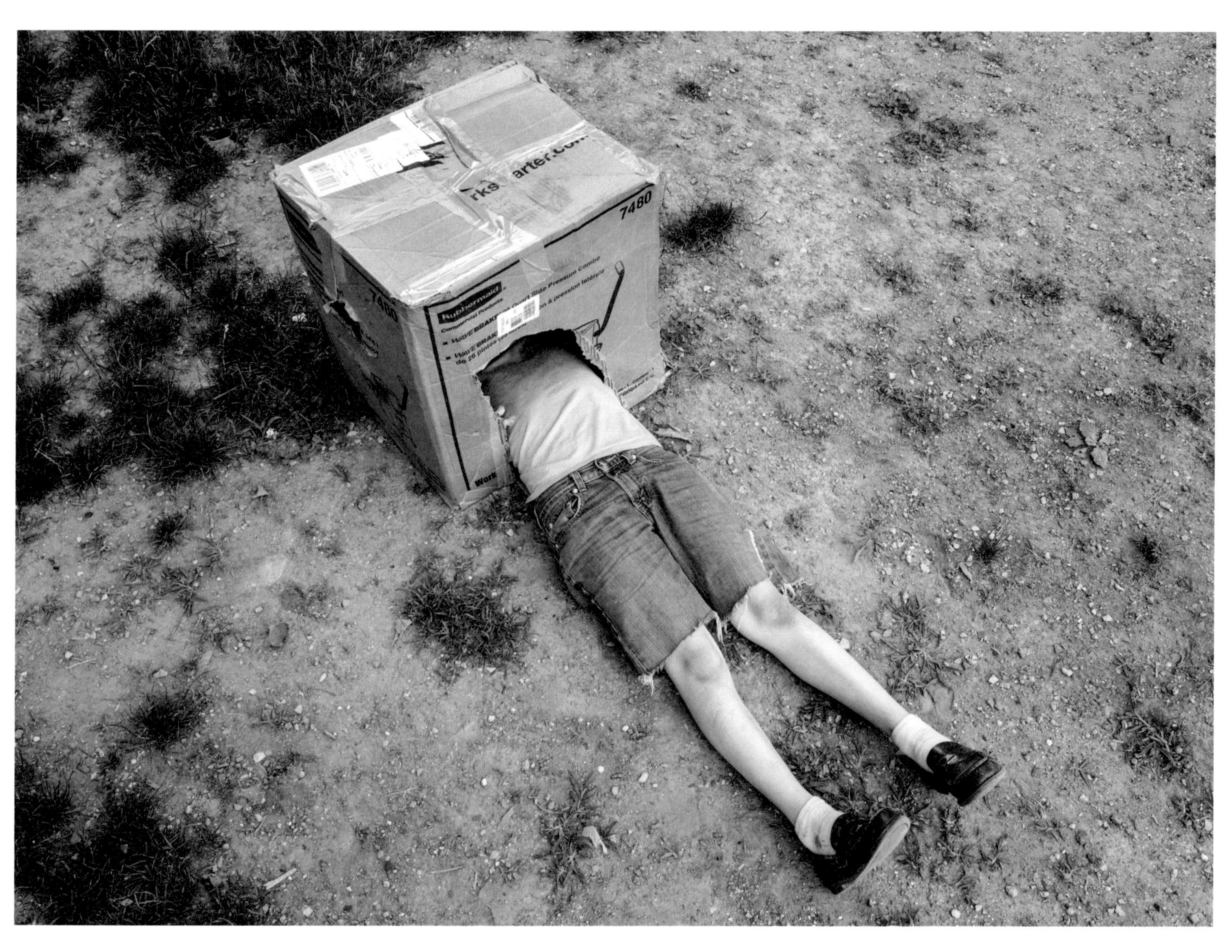
7480
7480
Rubbermaid

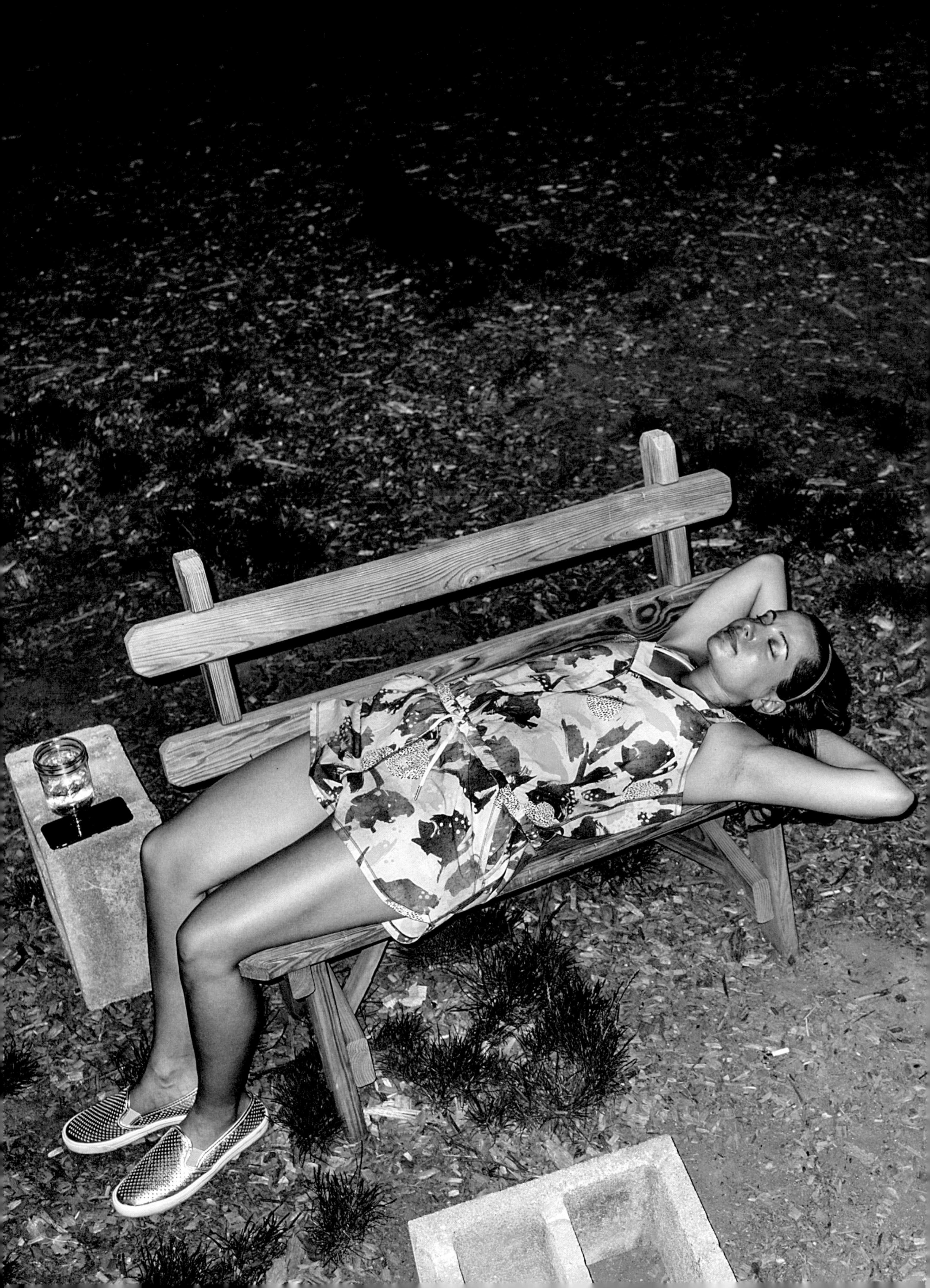

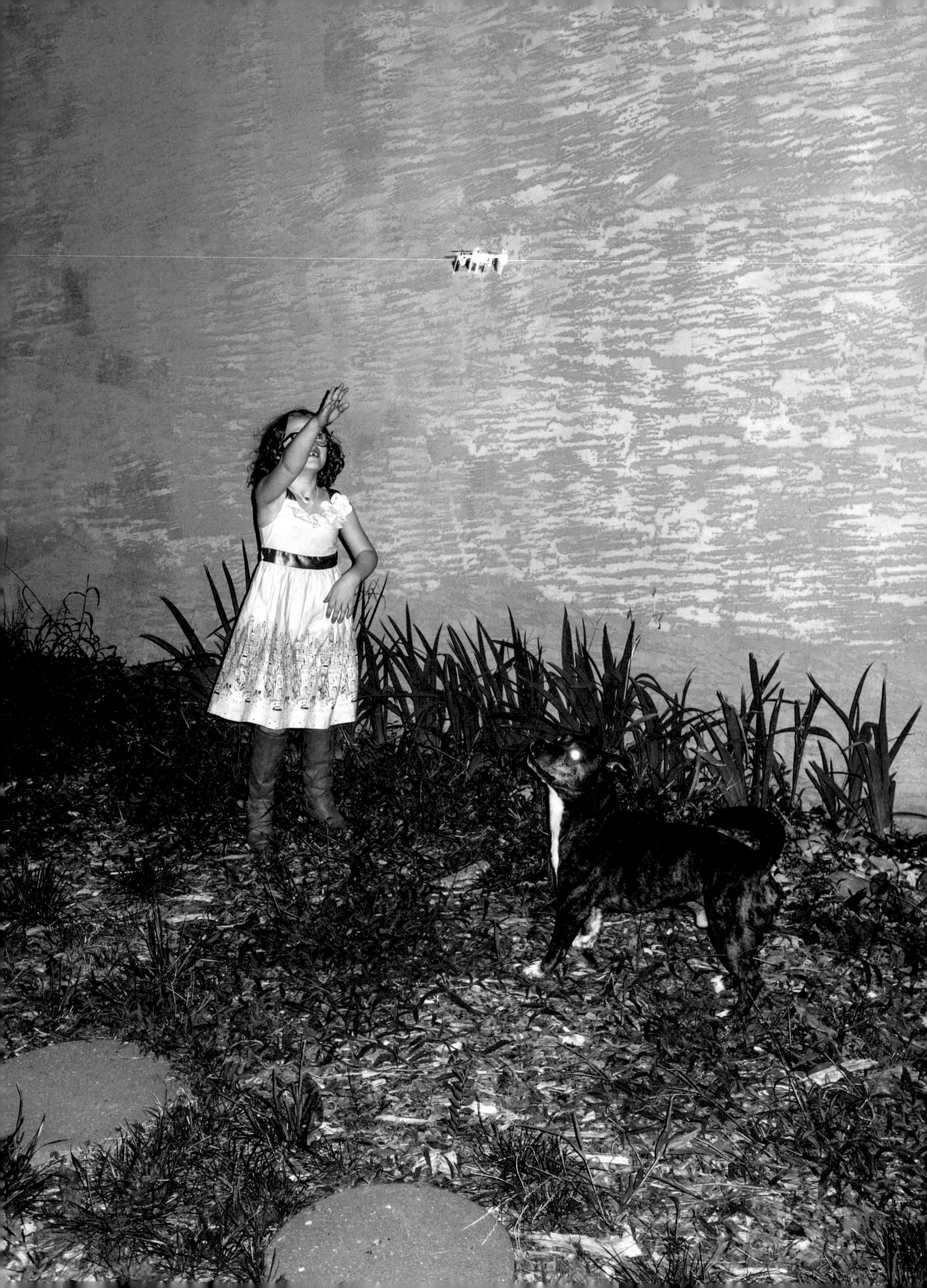

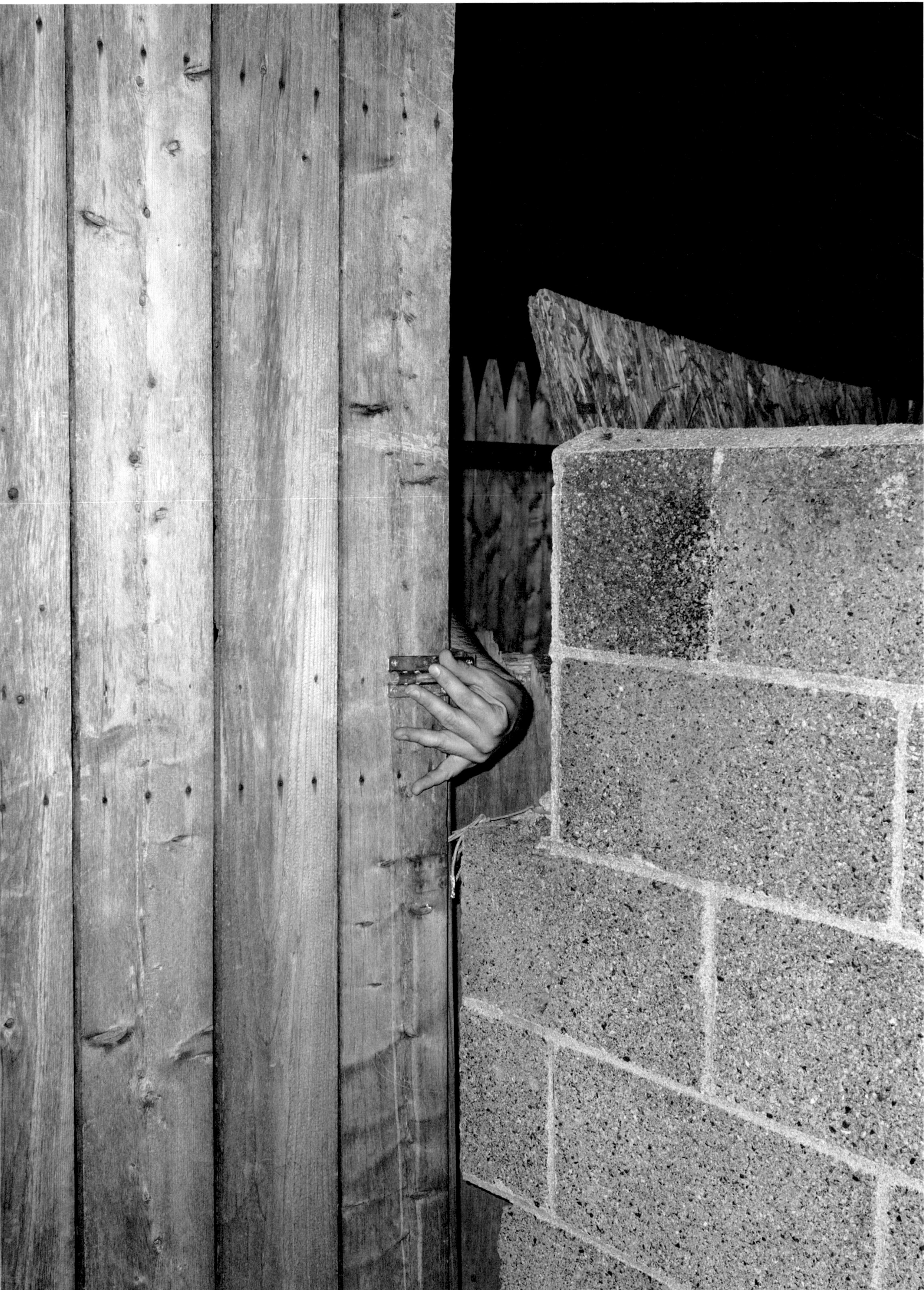

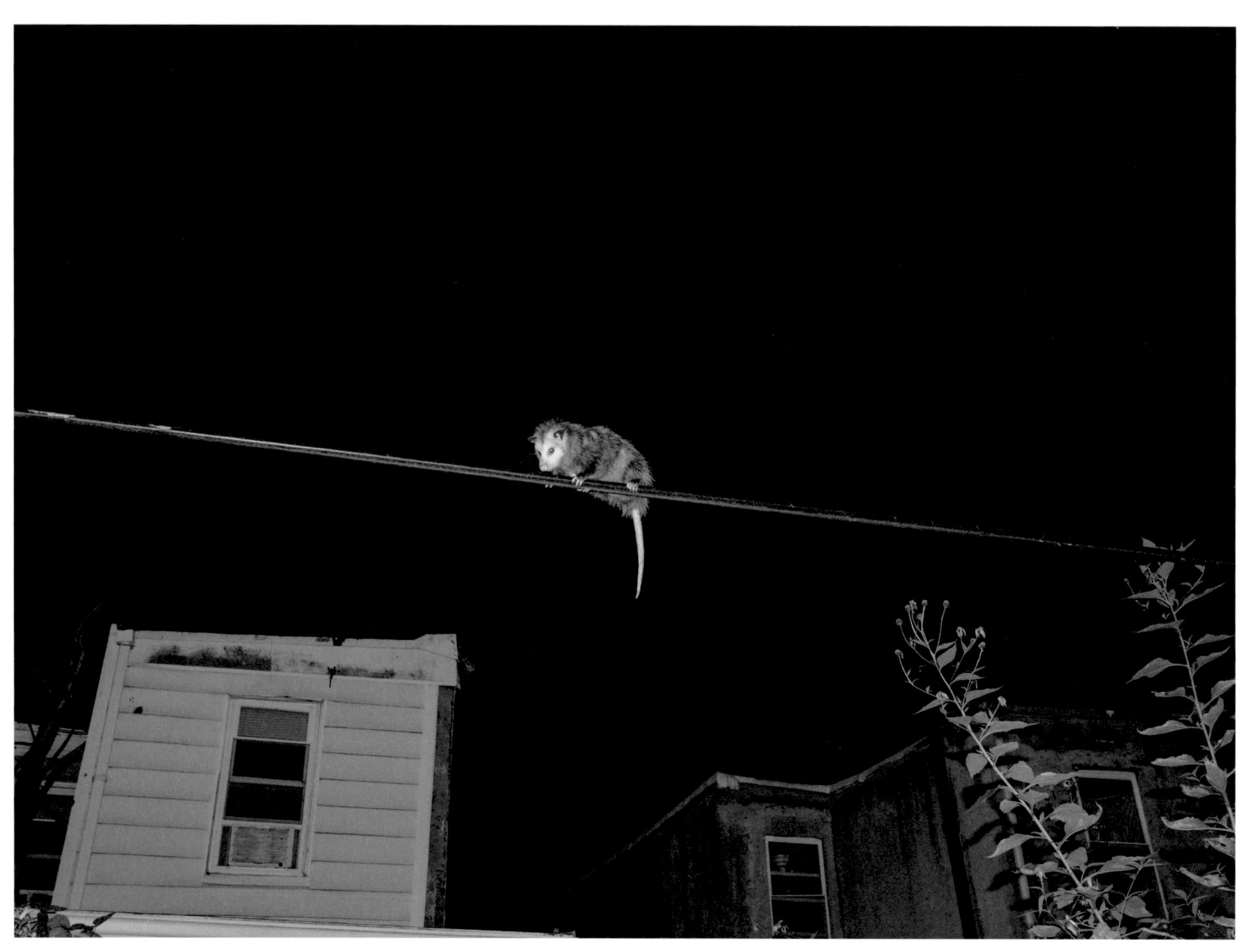

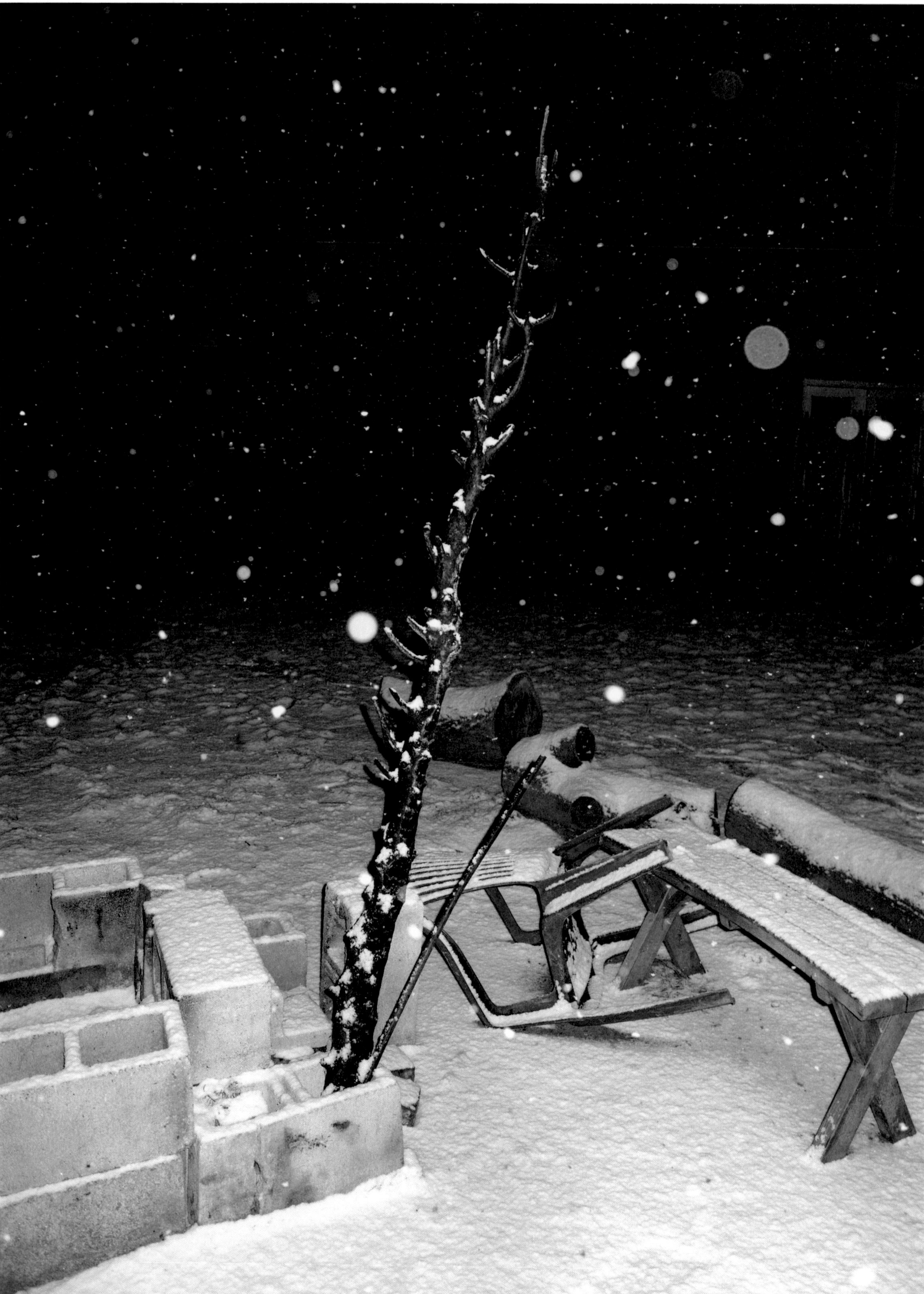

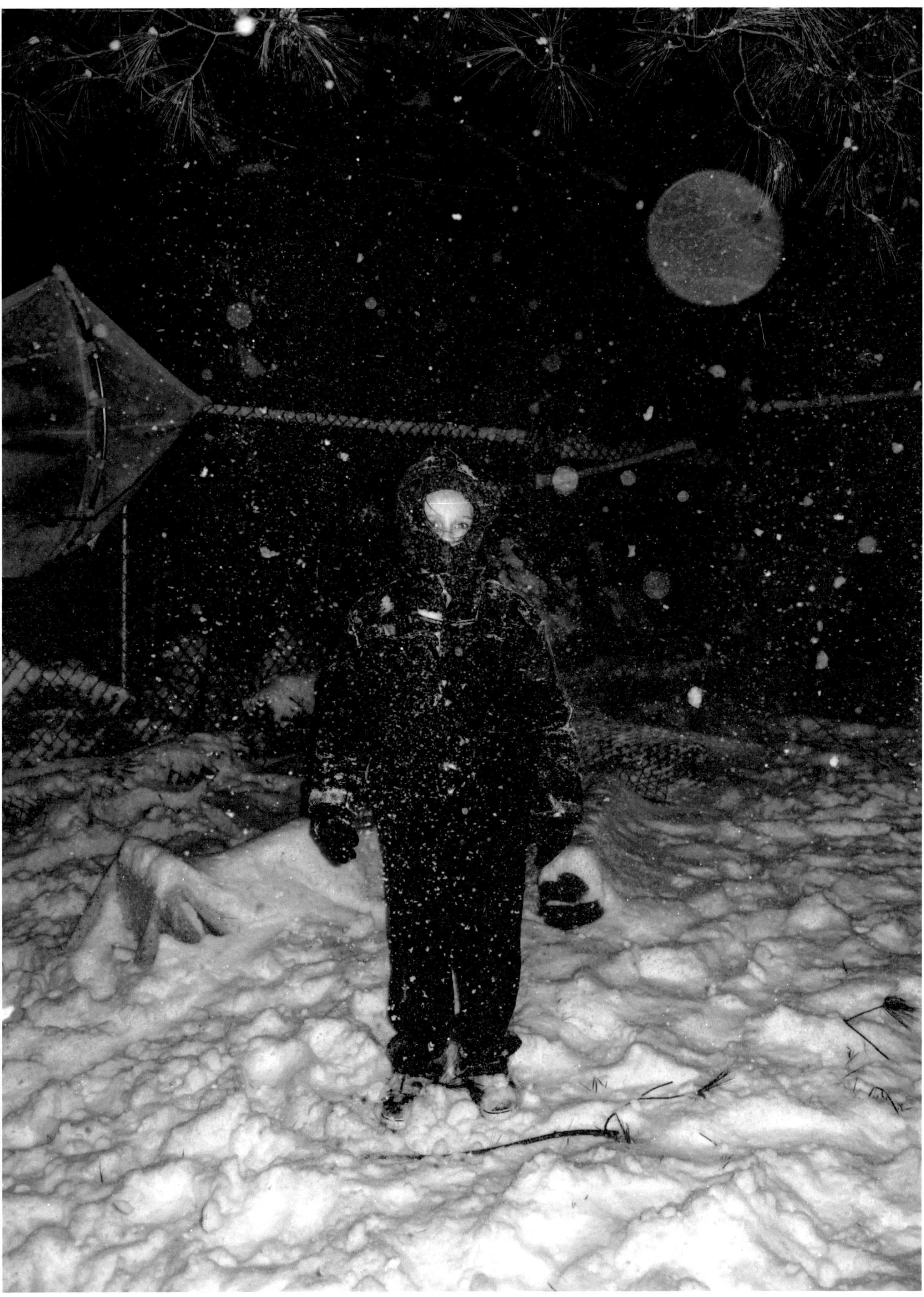

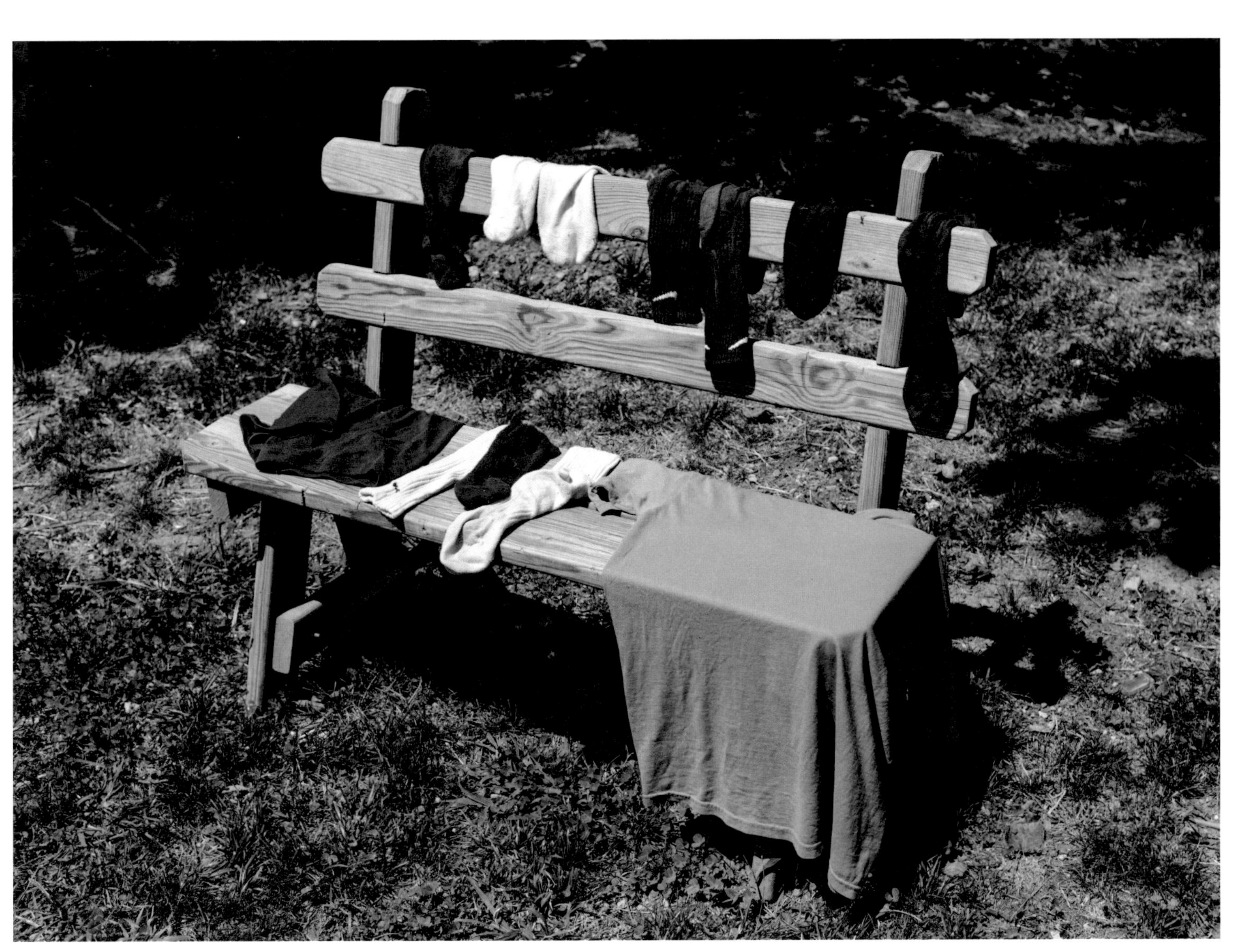

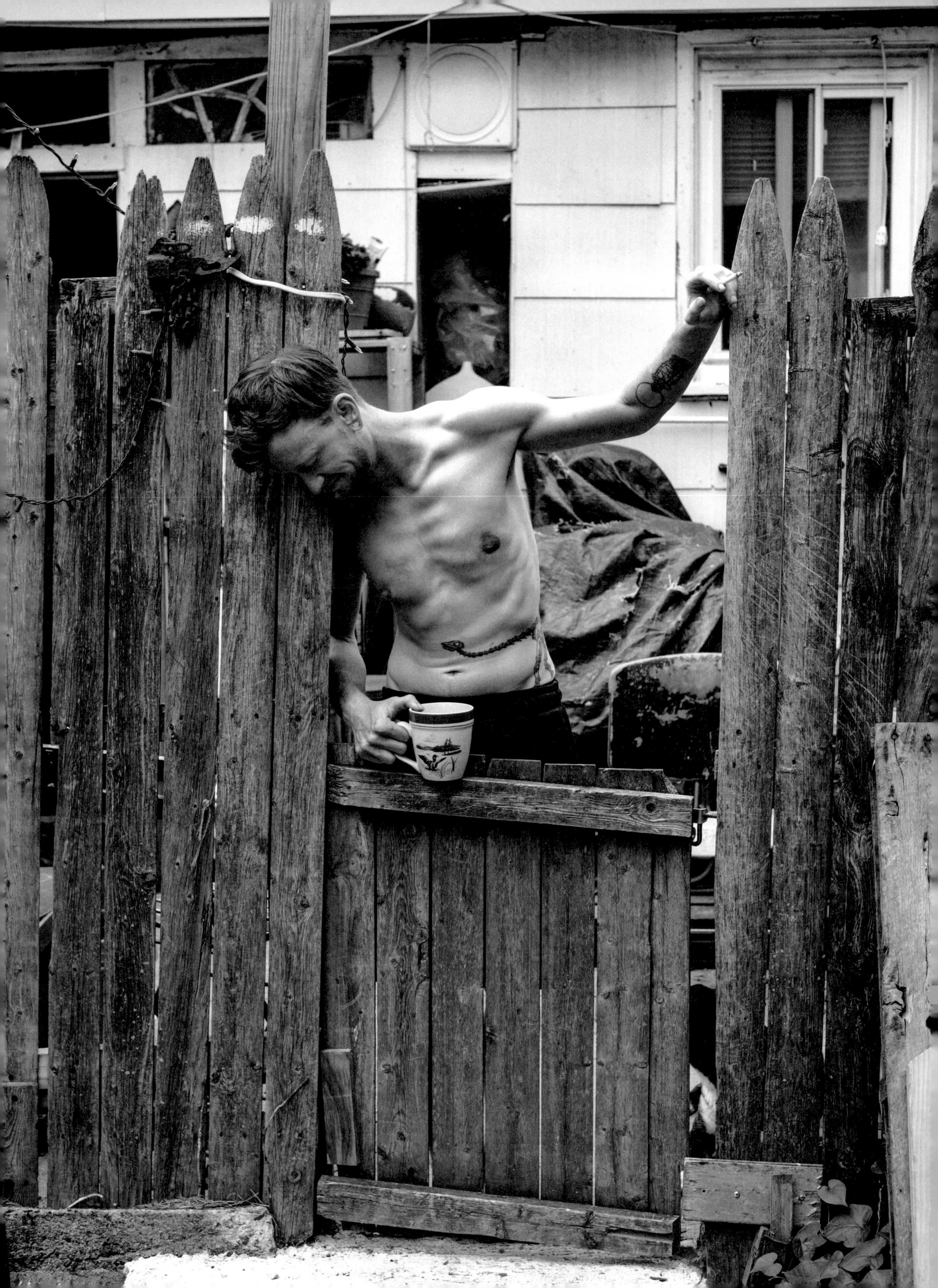

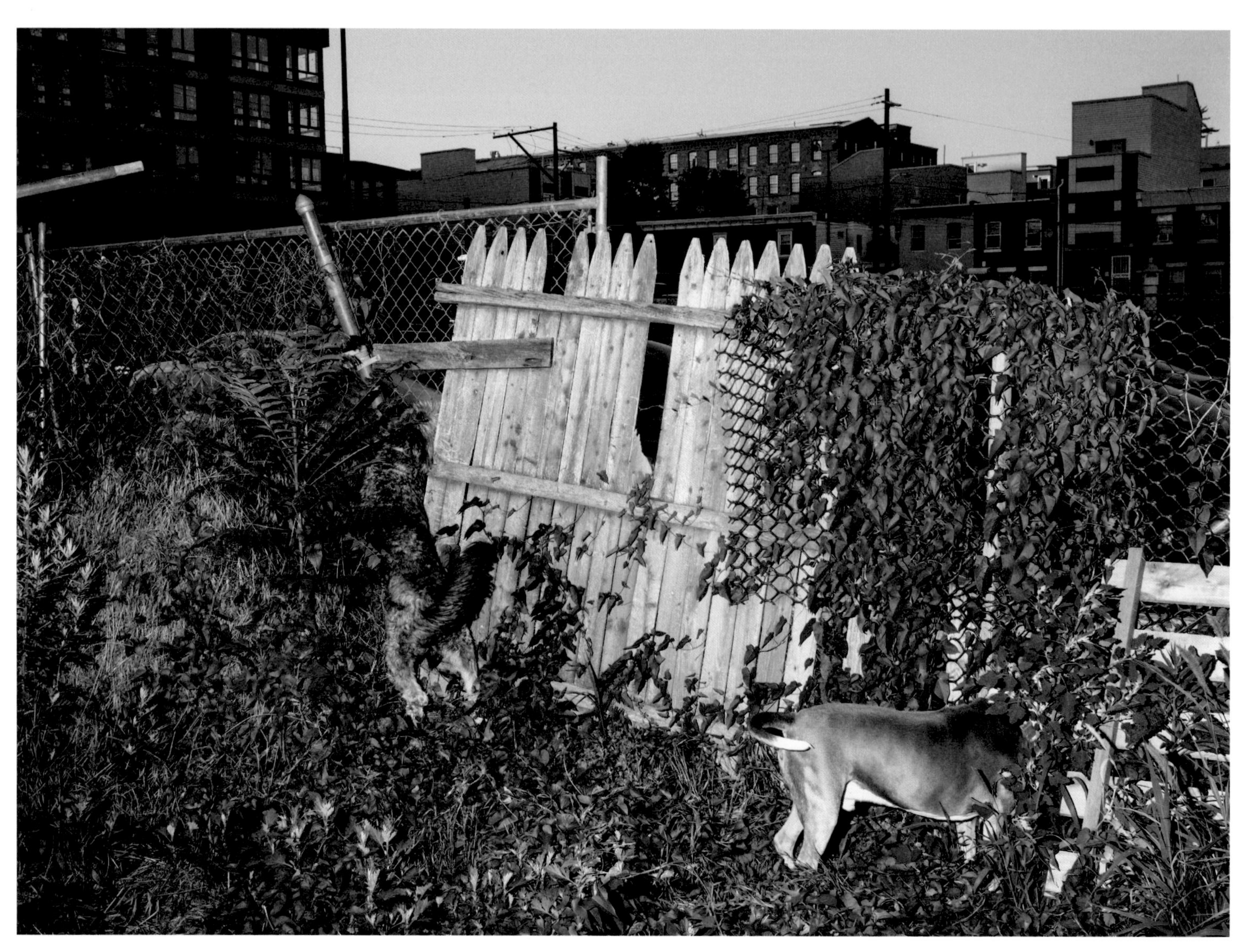

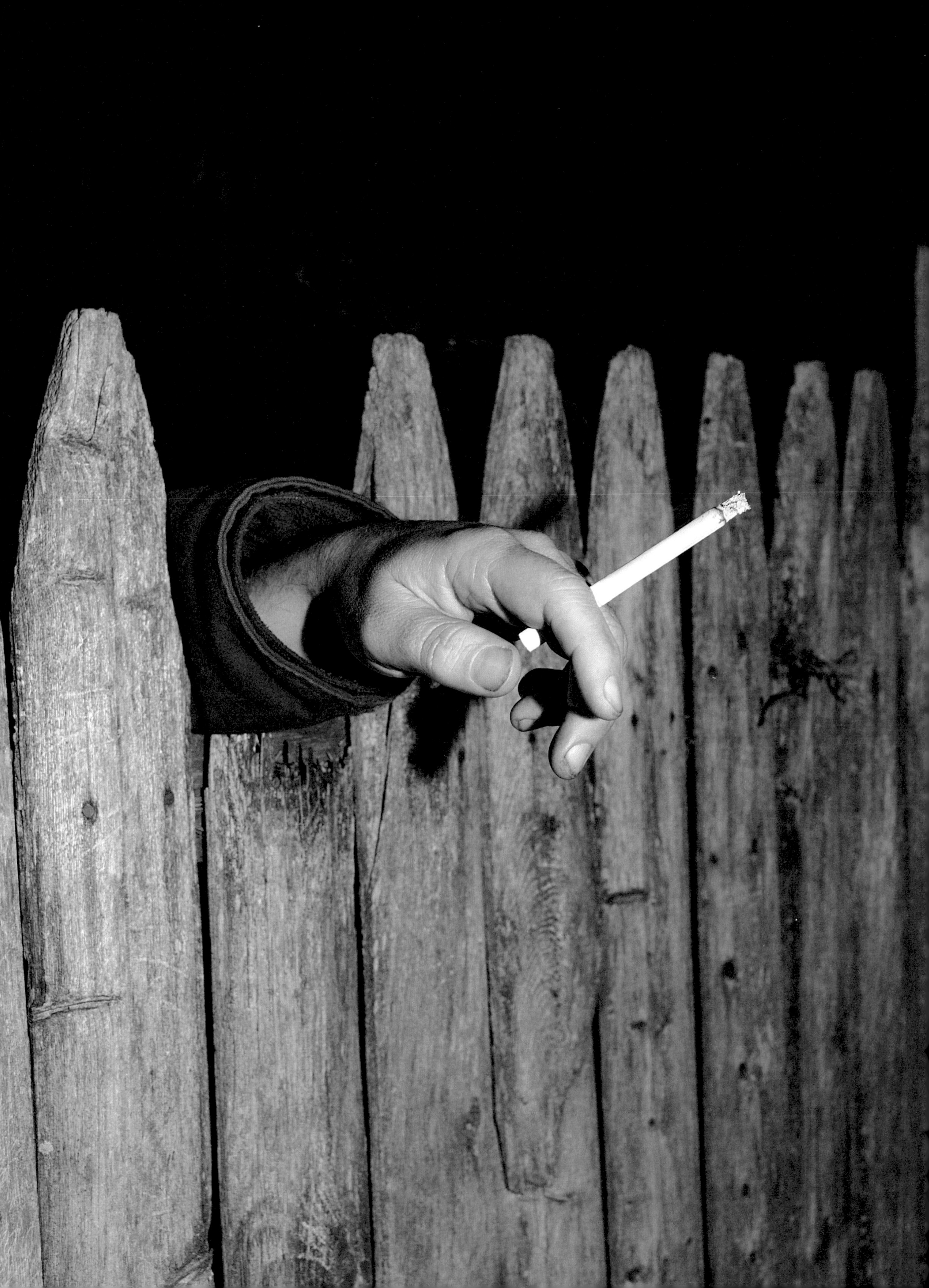

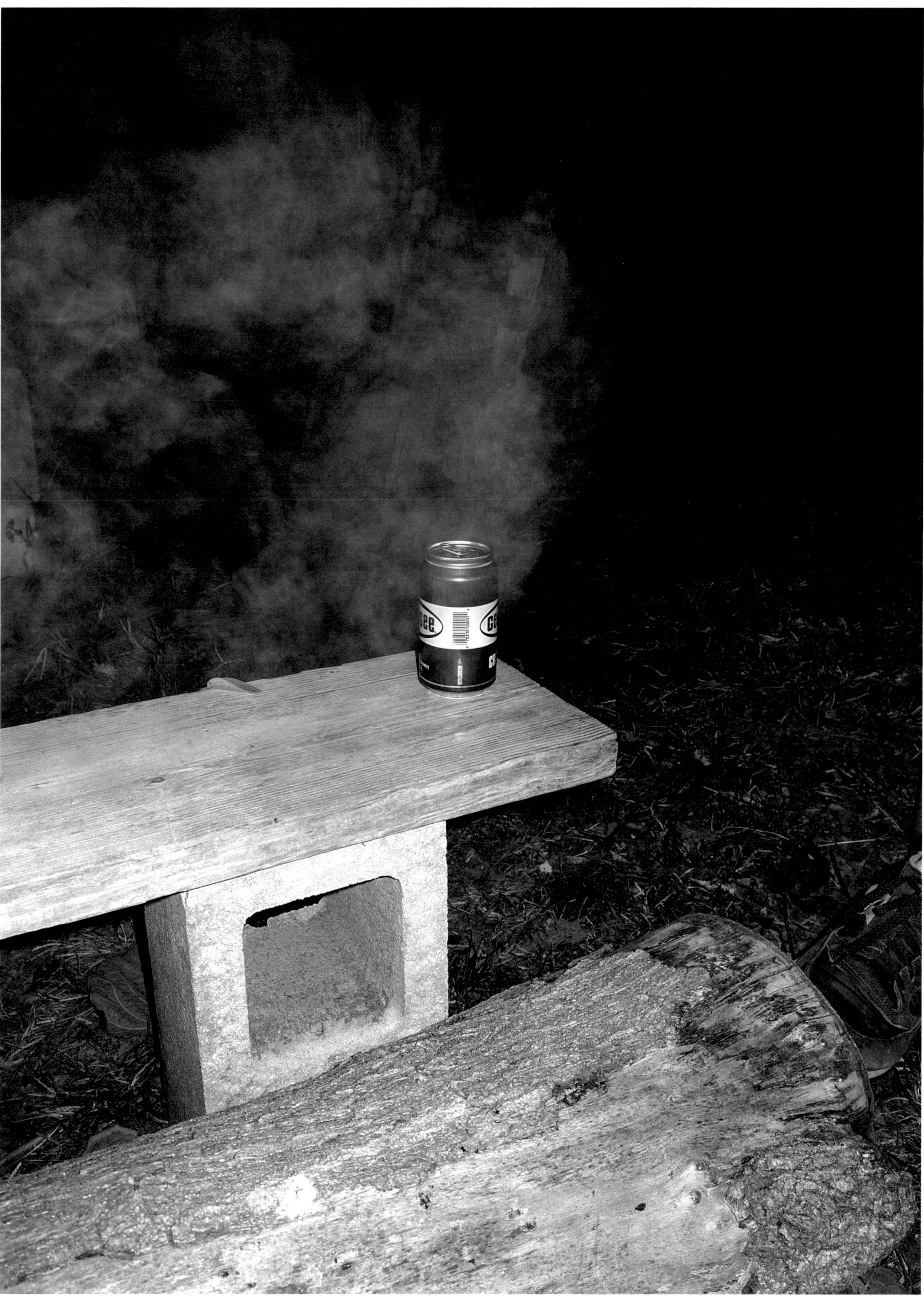

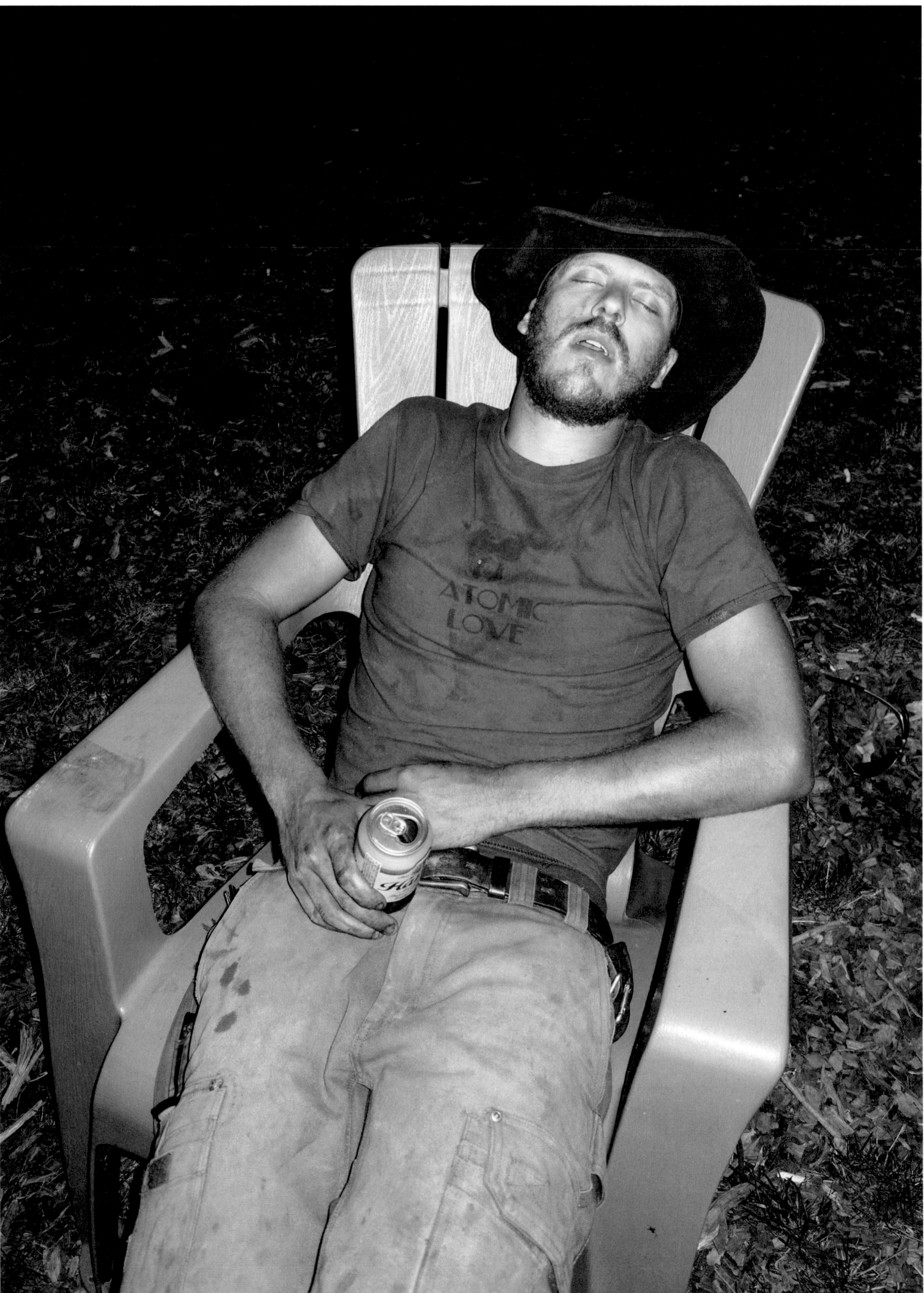
ATOMIC
LOVE

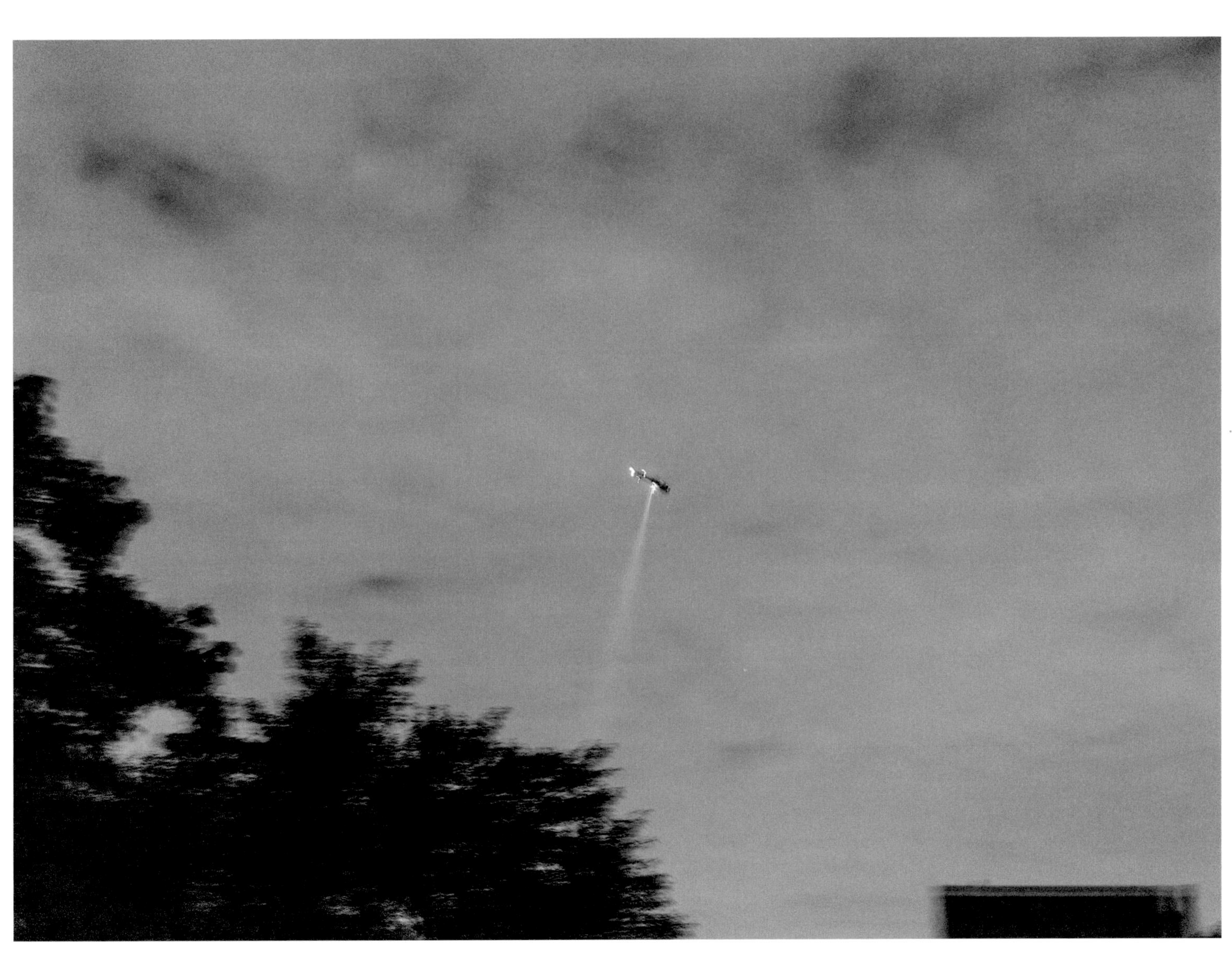

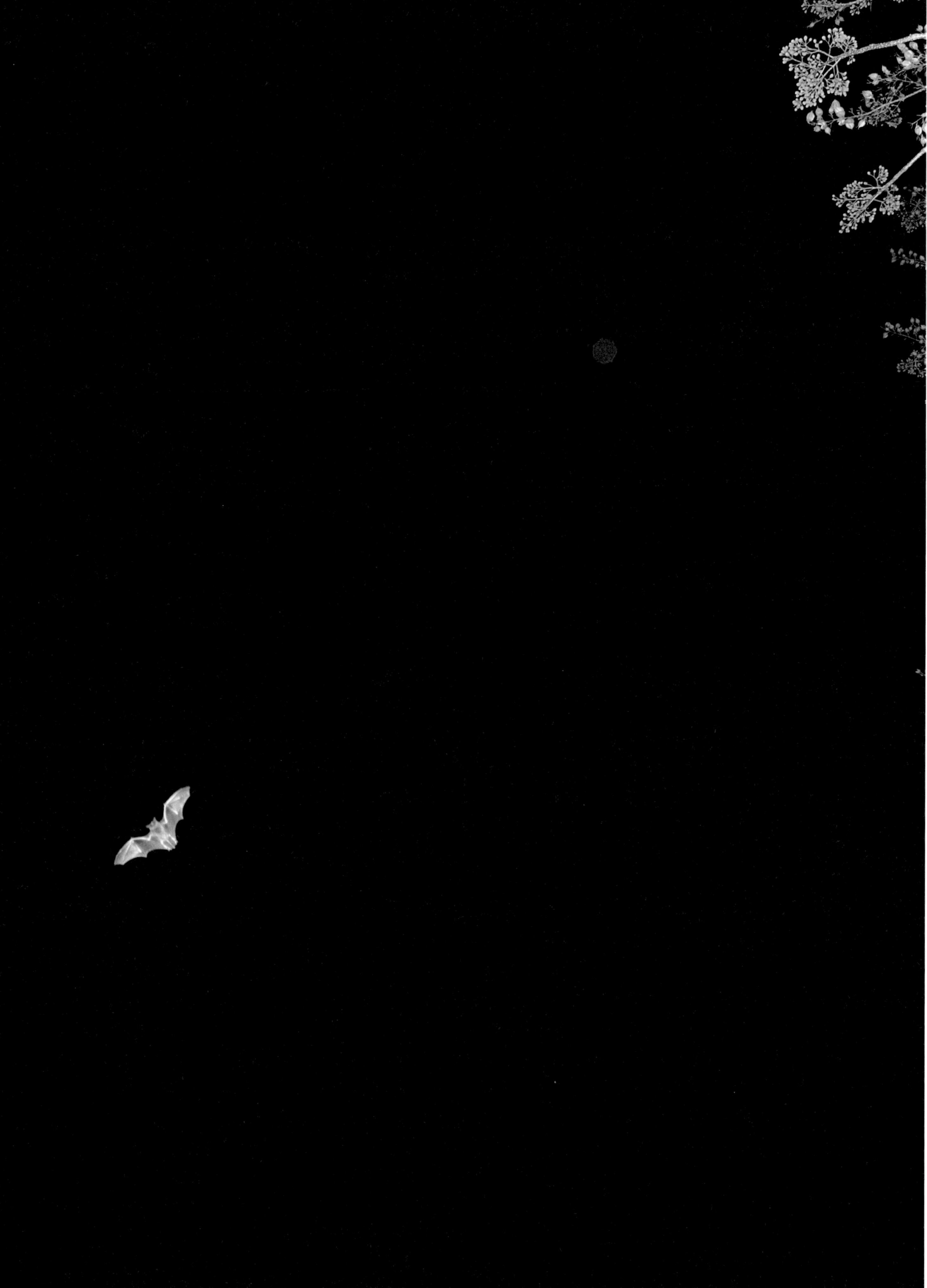

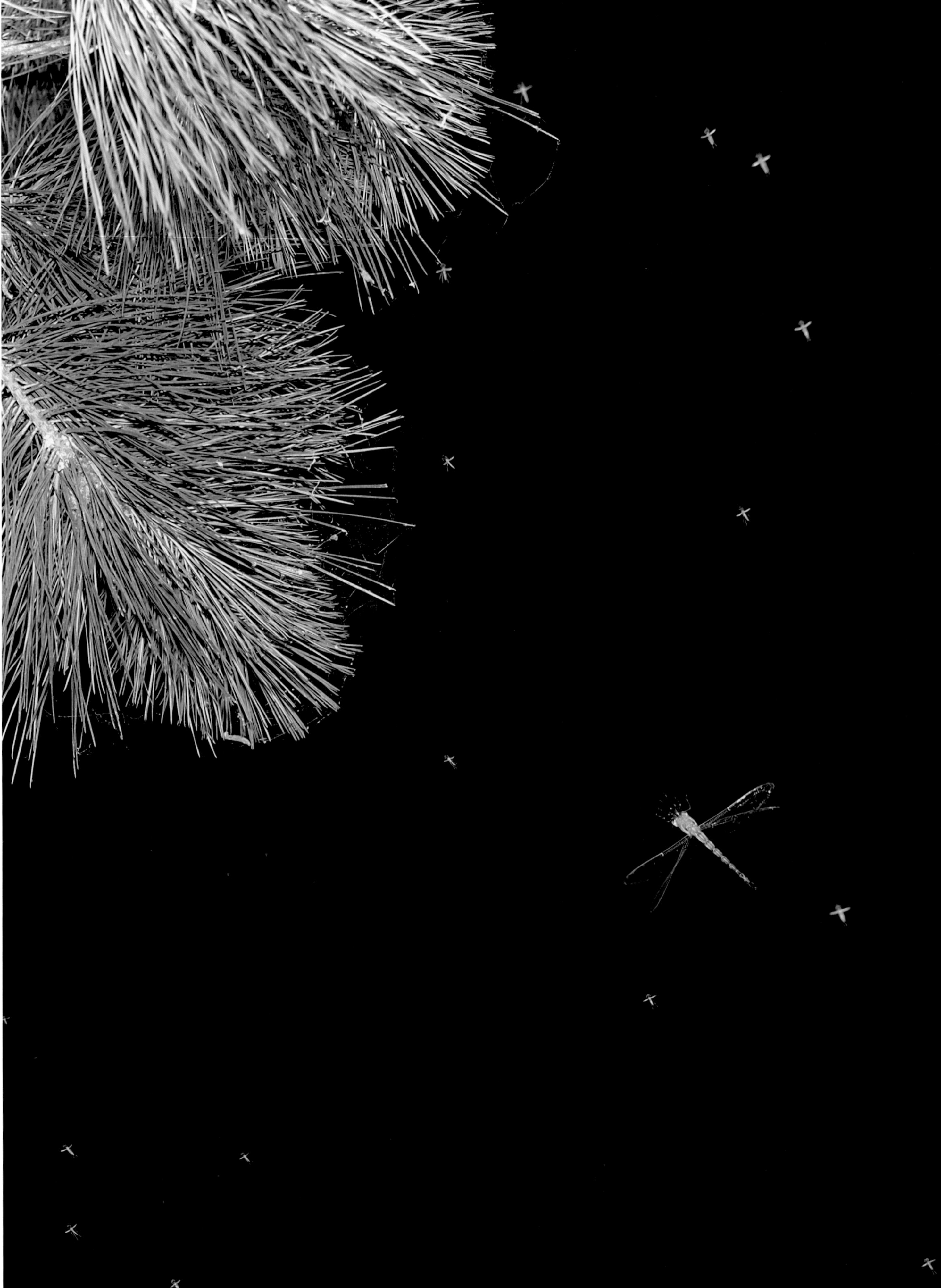

Fireworks mistaken for gunfire. Mother and son fighting at donut shop. Paper shredding truck on fire. Twins firing guns on train tracks. Man rammed with car. Group fight involving pepper spray, Tasers. Partially nude man in wheelchair brandishing knife. Black bear roaming in area. Knife displayed at gun fight. Woman setting clothes on fire. Man striking cars with nunchucks. Man throwing items inside Wawa. Massive cocaine shipment seized on cargo ship. People burglarizing home armed with gun, dogs, bat. Man lying down in drive through. Man throwing feces at cars. Man in fountain. Massive fire at Philadelphia Energy Solutions. Car stolen by 15 people. Person trapped in bag. Front door stolen. Women fighting with stun guns. Nude man running through Wawa parking lot. Woman injured after bug bomb exploded. Molotov cocktail thrown in attempted arson. Woman cut man with sword. Helmet-clad man threatening passerby with box cutter. Large deer disrupting traffic. Man with knife stabbing furniture. Man robbed in front of Wawa. Man threatened neighbor with machete. Woman robbed of hoverboard. Man brandishing shotgun at axe-wielder. Man resisting arrest at Wawa. Shoplifters carrying snake. Suspect broke into vehicle, sleeping. Woman's leg stuck in sewer grating. Man swinging pan in apartment. Officer struck by ATV. Group of people exposing themselves in park. Man with broken arm stealing from store. Woman stabbed by man armed with gun. Woman attempting to run down man who threw bricks at her. Man in American flag hat harassing people in front of cheesesteak shop. Cashier assaulted with tip jar. Sinkhole forming. Woman brandishing broken bottle outside Wawa. Security guard attempting to knife fight shoplifter. Glowing light. Two officers shot by active shooter. Four officers struck by active shooter. Five officers struck by active shooter. Six officers struck by active shooter. Robbery at art gallery. Man locked inside refrigerated vehicle. Man swimming in Delaware River. Three men in SUV armed with bow and arrow. Amazon truck stolen. Stabbing suspect hit by car. Flaming vehicle crashed into house. Beef jerky stolen by man with weed wacker. Thirty people fighting. Man swinging artificial leg at passerby. Car swerving with possible foot hanging from trunk. 18-20 people threatening Wawa employees. Report of 60 children fighting. Man shot 16 times, checked self into hospital. Sanitation division requested for large roadkill. Man jumping on counters at Wawa. Nude man broke into house, took shower. Woman stuck in tree. Woman carjacked by masked man in clown shoes. Kids armed with BB gun, throwing eggs. Report of woman with gun chasing egg throwers. Driver struck pole while attempting to strike pedestrian. Man stole entire supply of Red Bull, sandwiches from Wawa. Grenades recovered by bomb squad. Large injured opossum in the street. Group fleeing on stolen golf cart. Deer caught in weeds. Man riding horse abusively. Man in robot costume knocking on doors. Grenade found on train platform. Loose horse captured. Man stole door from home. Man dressed as priest reportedly breaking into home. Man in clown mask armed with shotgun. Report of man with rifle being chased by dog. Woman with purple hair kicked down basement door. Man in jumpsuit poured milk all over Frank Rizzo statue. Man stuck on fence after attempted break-in. Report of disputant wielding nail-studded stick. Man stole ten cans of Monster Energy Drink from Wawa. Attempted Christmas tree theft. Dump truck thief arrested. Report of two men dueling with metal pipes near loading dock. Kids assaulting juggler. Man robbed by twenty teenagers. Man wearing Trump mask attempting to rob bakery. Men in boat shooting animals along river. Twins armed with guns. Man throwing bottles at people, barking like dog. Roosters roaming street. Pit bull leaping from roof to roof. Drivers stopping to grab loose money on highway. Garage exploded. Assault with trash can at cheesesteak spot. White goat loose. Report of woman and child in car trapped in sinkhole. Person broke into home, cooked. Fifty people fighting. Person screaming. Refrigerator installation mistaken for ATM burglary. Crossing guard involved in fight with student. Report of men lighting firecrackers near vehicle gas tank. School evacuated twice after two bathroom fires, smoke bomb. Students and parents fighting outside school. Police sitting in park. Thirty person street fight. Two men fighting in an ice cream truck. Report of man armed with hammer, bow and arrow. Junkyard fire covers Center City in haze. Large group of parents and students fighting. Man attempting to take back stolen car. Group setting lawn on fire. Gun laying in street. Report of man hanging off side of house after woman stole ladder. Bleach thrown in fight involving ax. Series of small fires on train tracks. Person jumped out of ambulance. Report of man armed with bat fighting man armed with Wawa sign. Report of man in mini top hat armed with knife. Man breaking windows of cars mistaken for gunfire. Amazon driver car-jacked. Thieves in disguise as police stole wallet. Report of driver armed with tranquilizer gun. Man sitting in middle of intersection. Report of beef stolen at gunpoint. Report of man swinging samurai sword. Man in custody after firing shots at targets inside home. Report of man throwing objects at people at the University of the Arts. Assault with fireworks. Report of man in clown mask firing paintball guns. Report of man cracking whip. Report of burning bush. Report of man stabbed in back. Portable toilet on fire. Police vehicle on fire. Objects thrown at police. Report of people holding crowbars. Items thrown at police. Protesters erecting barricades. Protestors outside police headquarters. Fire at Starbucks. Mandatory curfew declared in Philadelphia. People burglarizing businesses. Building fire. Two-alarm fire. People burglarizing strip mall. Police activity related to looting. Crowd throwing rocks, bottles at police officers. Three-alarm fire. Fire in pawn shop. People looting vodka factory. Man stole coin safe from bank. Van driver handing out hammers to children. Report of commercial burglary with hammers. Civilian has two burglary suspects locked in garage. People breaking into zoo. Report of loose tiger. Man critically injured by ATM explosion in front of sports bar. ATM blown open in wooded area. Firecracker detonated in outhouse. Person robbed of black Tesla at gunpoint. Report of woman armed with bug spray making threats at Wawa. Report of man weaponizing hoverboard. Reports of shots fired near drag race. Vicious dog forcing man to stay stuck on roof. Woman with dynamite in bag detained by police. Man flashed gun, stole red roses from gas station. Nude woman jumped in, sped off with white Jaguar. Three men trapped in raft on Delaware River. Report of armed dispute over fireworks. Burning vehicle struck building. Car fire in front of zoo. Report of man armed with three machetes. Man pushing stolen piano down the sreet. Car stuck in sinkhole. Report of 15 people fighting with Tasers. Knife duel in street. Man standing dangerously close to edge of roof. Report of drones ramming people on hotel roof. Woman in cow costume harassing Wawa employees. Pit bull attacking person on roof. Report of five shotgun-wielding man. Casino machine robbed in three-man heist. Balloons popping mistaken for gunfire. Mattress factory fire. Raccoon chasing man. Man stuck in vent. Report of people fighting in voting line. Woman assaulted, poll worker injured. Report of people fighting at poll site. Dispute over political shirt. Man causing disturbance at poll site. Exploding ATM. Roof fire at gentlemen's club. Undetonated hand grenades found in church. Nude man dancing in street. Report of man and woman armed with barbed wire bat. Armed robbery suspect shot by customer. Report of woman armed with five frying pans. Man beaten unconscious after stabbing person. Horse, pit bull detained. Large fight at Wawa. Bus drove into sinkhole. Man refusing to leave house on fire.

In colonial era Philadelphia, Benjamin Franklin brought together a group of diverse individuals to meet for the purpose of mutual improvement. They would gather in a tavern to debate questions of morals, politics, current events, philosophy, and local businesses. In 2013 Philly, a much less formal group of neighbours came together in the large vacant lot behind our houses. When we gathered, we would talk for hours—often arguing the absurdity of human existence while our phone notifications alerted us to crimes in the area as they happened in real time. The harshness of the world was cushioned by the support of community. And, because of that, we improved the quality of each other's lives tenfold.

This book is for my neighbours, both past and present. 1921 - Sawyer, Lego (RIP), Caleb, Alex, Chelsea, Lady, Raven, Dave, Mikey, Ali, Alexis, Ella. 1917 - Sadie, Zach, Amy, Goose, Scout (RIP), Kris Lee, Nate. 1915 - Michael, Katie, Raisin. 1928 - Tom, Laura, John, Johnny, Jackson, Devyn, John, Owen, Harris, Skye. 1926 - Joe, Bethany, Jayden, Mya, Roger, Leo, Kate, Elianna, Jak (RIP), and all other friends, neighbours, and family that have visited our lot. Shoutout to the Philadelphia Land Bank and the negligent property owners who, without their knowledge, allowed a community to flourish.

No work is or has ever been created in a bubble. I'm grateful for the friendship and guidance of Sophie Barbasch, Ian Bates, Jackie Bates, David Billet, J Carrier, Tim Carpenter, Nelson Chan, Jesse Chan, Jenny Drumgoole, Matt Eich, Paul Farber, Taylor Galloway, Jennifer Garza-Cuen, Jezabeth Gonzalez, Christopher Gianunzio, Kris Graves, Joshua Dudley Greer, CJ Harker, Natalie Ivis, Ian Kline, Pedro Letria, Anne Massoni, Andrea Modica, Jay Muhlin, Kyle Myles and Tori Hardy, Anna Neighbor, Ted Partin, Jake Reinhart, David Rothenberg, Steven B Smith, Jared Soares, Lindsay Sparagana, Chad States, Mark Power and Keith Yahrling. My greatest appreciation is for my wife, Anne Erickson, who is a constant source of support and inspiration. I carry you all with me.

Thank you Stuart Smith, Katie Clifford, Claudia Paladini and everyone at GOST for their patience, sensitivity, and thoughtfulness in bringing this love letter to print. Without you all, this dirtbag Narnia wouldn't have left the wardrobe.

Massive thank you to Will Vogt, Gabriel Angemi, Dominic Episcopo, Ryan Hancock, and Melanie Bilenker for their continued and generous support of my work.

Much love to my Pizza Shackamaxon family—you've given me a second lease on life. Fuck academia forever.

Philadelphia, you mean everything to me.

The Group For Mutual Improvement
First published in 2024
by GOST Books, London

info@gostbooks.com
gostbooks.com

Text compiled by Jordan Baumgarten

Edited and designed by GOST:
Rossella Castello, Katie Clifford,
Gemma Gerhard, Justine Hucker,
Allon Kaye, Eleanor Macnair,
Claudia Paladini, Ana Rocha

Printed in Italy by EBS

British Library cataloguing-in-publication data. A catalogue record of this book is available from the British Library.

ISBN 978-1-915423-32-0